A Shared Vision

The Garman Ryan Collection
at The New Art Gallery Walsall

A Shared Vision

The Garman Ryan Collection
at The New Art Gallery Walsall

Sheila McGregor

with an introduction by Kitty Godley

and commentaries by Oliver Buckley

MERRELL

First published in 1999 by
Merrell Publishers Limited
42 Southwark Street, London SE1 1UN
www.merrellpublishers.com

Reprinted 2001

Distributed in the USA and Canada by Rizzoli International Publications, Inc.
through St Martin's Press, 175 Fifth Avenue, New York, New York 10010

British Library Cataloguing-in-Publication Data
McGregor, Sheila
A shared vision : the Garman Ryan collection at The New Art Gallery Walsall
1.Garman, Kathleen – Art collections 2.Ryan, Sally – Art collections 3.Art – Exhibitions
I.Title II.Garman Ryan Collection III New Art Gallery (Walsall, England)
708.2'492

ISBN 1 85894 086 9 (hardback)
ISBN 1 85894 101 6 (paperback)

Edited by Julian Honer

Designed by Tim Harvey

Printed and bound in Italy

Front cover: Amedeo Modigliani, *Caryatid (Cariatide)*, 1913–14 (detail; see plate 6)

Half-title: Jacob Epstein, *Heads of the New York Madonna and Child, ca.* 1926–27 (see fig. 23, p. 31)

Frontispiece: The New Art Gallery Walsall, designed by Caruso St John Architects, 1997–99
(photograph by Hélène Binet)

Contents

Preface

As the Managing Director of Birmingham International Airport, I am delighted that our company is associated with the publication of the first fully illustrated catalogue of the Garman Ryan Collection. Since it opened to the public in Walsall in 1974, the collection has been one of the region's best-kept secrets – a treasure-trove of paintings, drawings, sculpture and artefacts from all corners of the world, hidden away above the library in the centre of Walsall. From now on, in its new world-class home, this collection is certain to attract visitors from far and wide. Some of them, we hope, will use Birmingham International Airport.

Every year the airport brings tens of thousands of travellers to the West Midlands, either *en route* for other places or, increasingly, heading for destinations within the region itself. The reasons are by no means solely commercial. To the region's traditional industries and familiar tourist attractions must now be added some of the most vibrant cultural amenities in the country: music-making, theatre, ballet and art galleries to rival the best in Europe.

Birmingham International Airport has recently embarked on a ten-year expansion programme, which will result in greatly enhanced facilities and capacity. The creation of a new home for the Garman Ryan Collection in Walsall is just one example of the parallel investment currently being made in the region's cultural infrastructure. We are pleased to support this far-sighted initiative through sponsorship of the Garman Ryan Collection catalogue. In so doing, we acknowledge the vital role that the arts can play in regeneration and the importance of working in partnership with other agencies to achieve a better future for the West Midlands.

Brian Summers
Managing Director

This book has also been made possible by generous support from:
The Paul Mellon Centre for Studies in British Art
Adrian and Susan Cadbury

Foreword

Having once discovered the Garman Ryan Collection, visitors invariably want to come back for a longer and closer look. For however much you think you know this collection, it retains the power to take you by surprise. Artists love it because of what it tells them about the way that other artists think; children respond immediately to the rich array of animal subjects, landscapes and portraits; all who get to know the collection are enthralled by the story of Kathleen Garman, Jacob Epstein and Sally Ryan. For too long, however, the collection has been well known only to a local audience. Now, for the first time, the publication of this catalogue enables us to share the many pleasures of the Garman Ryan Collection with a wider public across the world.

The opening of The New Art Gallery on Walsall's Town Wharf provides a world-class home for the Garman Ryan Collection as well as exhibition galleries, education spaces and visitor facilities of international quality. The spirit of the Garman Ryan Collection – intimate, adventurous and eclectic – has been a powerful inspiration to architects Caruso St John in their creation of a gallery conceived as a series of house-like spaces, some large and majestic, others smaller in scale and more informal. The gallery's many windows, which offer some of the most breathtaking views to be found anywhere in the region, make a journey through the building something to remember.

For Kathleen Garman the route to personal and professional fulfilment lay in London. By giving something back to Walsall, however, she hoped to improve in some small way the cultural life of her native Black Country. Thirty years on, the UK Arts Lottery and European structural funds have enabled the construction of a new home for her collection. A long-awaited programme of capital investment in the arts is bringing about a startling reconfiguration of the British cultural map. The publication of this catalogue will, we hope, draw national and international attention to one of the newest landmarks on that map and one of the projects by which the Arts Lottery programme will surely be remembered. Our title, *A Shared Vision*, aptly describes not just the collecting partnership that Kathleen Garman enjoyed with Sally Ryan, but also the aspiration of Walsall's New Art Gallery to bring art, artists and audiences into an ever closer, more enriching and more sustainable relationship.

Peter Jenkinson
Director, The New Art Gallery Walsall

Acknowledgements

The combined efforts of a large number of people, over many years, have made this publication possible. We particularly wish to thank Kitty Godley, whose recollections bring vividly and graciously to life the context in which the collection of her mother, Kathleen Garman, was made. Other members of the Epstein and Garman families have generously shared their memories with us and supported the development of Walsall Museums and Art Gallery Service in numerous ways: notably Jackie and Isabel Epstein, Annabel Freud, Anne Freud, Gerald Garman, William Garman, Wynne Godley, Beth Lipkin and the late Michael Wishart. On the Ryan side of the collection, we are indebted to Sally Ryan's niece, The Countess of Airlie, and to Saville Ryan-Marsh and Theodore Ryan Robb. We also warmly acknowledge the contribution made to the project by Antonia Payne, whose extensive research for an earlier version of this catalogue between 1990 and 1992 yielded information and insights that have underpinned all subsequent discussion of the collection. Her findings have closely informed the introductory essay. Among the other scholars, curators and researchers who have provided assistance are Brian Allen, Judith Collins, Penelope Curtis, Terry Friedman, Malcolm McLeod, June Rose, Evelyn Silber, Michael Tooby, Richard Verdi and Giles Waterfield. Two recent volunteers, Rebecca Tate Lovery and Grace Brockington, have also done much to further our knowledge of Sally Ryan's life and work, while many of those who knew Jacob Epstein and Kathleen Garman have kindly allowed their memories to be recorded for the Gallery's fast-growing Epstein Archive, among them Clive Beardsmore, Ralph and Caroline Brown, Stephen Gardiner, Josef Herman, Geoffrey Ireland, Rosie Price (née Newbould), Ian Seymour-Wells, Frank and Kathleen Ward and Alice Weldon. Previous Keepers of Fine Art, Peter Vigurs, Valerie Millington and Lindsey Brooks, have all played an important part in documenting the collection. Gallery technicians Rob Allen and Mike Gallagher efficiently co-ordinated the photography of individual works, while the photography itself has been undertaken, at different times, by Anthony Barthorpe and Gary Kirkham. Special thanks are owed to Simon Hucker for patiently producing the catalogue of works; to Sue McNally for her invaluable long-term research on the ethnographic material in the collection and on copyright; to Deborah Lote and the Gallery's Visitor Assistant team for administrative and moral support; to Andrew Davies for his fund-raising efforts; to Oliver Buckley for his lively analysis of individual pieces; to Laura Regan and Kate Travers for cataloguing assistance; and above all to the Keeper of Fine Art, Jo Digger, whose enthusiasm for and knowledge of the collection is an inspiration to colleagues and visitors alike. With the active support of A. David Owen and his fellow members of the Walsall Museums and Art Galleries Development Trust, we have at last raised the money to make a catalogue of the Garman Ryan Collection a reality. Our thanks must finally go to the individuals and organizations whose funding has enabled the production of this landmark publication: The Paul Mellon Centre for Studies in British Art, Adrian and Susan Cadbury and Birmingham International Airport.

Peter Jenkinson and
Sheila McGregor
1999

The Garman Ryan Collection: As I Saw It

Kitty Godley

It was after the death in 1959 of my father, the sculptor Jacob Epstein, that my mother (née Kathleen Garman) and Sally Ryan, an American sculptor who was my father's only pupil and a friend of both my parents, had to consider the serious problem of how to house or store the large collection of paintings, prints, drawings, sculpture and artefacts that they had collected together, largely over the previous decade.

My mother had been left with my father's huge house in Hyde Park Gate, London, with his studio abutting on to a mews at the back. She understandably wanted to move to somewhere smaller and more convenient. Even then, after the sale of his enormous collection of ethnographic works – mainly African carvings and sculptures, some antique jewellery, New Zealand tikis and other artefacts – in accordance with his will, there would not be room for the residue in Elm Park Road in Chelsea, where she had moved after the sale of my father's house.

One of my father's collection, a beautiful sandstone temple dancer, was sold to the British Museum, and a cabinet of ethnographic objects was donated to the Garman Ryan Collection, together with the beautiful mask of Nefertiti bequeathed by my father to my mother, possibly because he saw a likeness to her in the Nefertiti profile (fig. 1).

My mother's first thought for a gallery site was of her old childhood home and birthplace, Oakeswell Hall (fig. 2), in the Black Country, where she had been brought up with her eight siblings – two brothers and six sisters. It was an ancient manor house dating from the fourteenth century and lived in by my grandparents, Dr Walter Chancellor Garman and his wife Marjorie Frances, my beloved grandmother. It was in a little village called Wednesbury, now swallowed up in the West Midlands conurbation, and had an avenue of elms and extensive gardens and grounds.

When my mother impulsively made a journey to visit her old home, she was surprised and shocked to find that it had been demolished; there was nothing there but a building site and a few skips. Only the tall stone gateposts surmounted with stone balls were left standing – the Elm Avenue all cut down.

The only living relative she had in Walsall was Gerald Garman, a nephew, the son of Bernard, Dr Walter Garman's brother, so it was to him she turned for help.

After some negotiations, the Old Library in the municipal centre of Walsall was thought to be suitable for her and Sally's purposes. It was a turn-of-the-century stone building set in a secluded and leafy street away from the main traffic, and the two friends' very diverse, familial and wide-ranging collection remained

Sir Jacob Epstein, *Portrait of Kitty* (detail), 1937, pencil, 56 × 43.5 cm
(22⅛ × 17⅛ in.), GR.70

there until the creation of The New Art Gallery. It was not ideal because it was badly lit and there was not enough wall space, although this was much improved by the dynamic new curator Peter Jenkinson.

But for me, the genesis and nucleus of this collection began in the mid-1930s – to be exact, in my mother's house in Chelsea, at 272 King's Road, later to be demolished during the Festival of Britain in 1951 to make way for a new fire station. It once was a terrace of shabby but elegant houses with graceful wrought-iron balconies giving on to a long garden at the back and the King's Road in front.

Many of the artefacts now in Walsall were in the double drawing room – for instance the Cameroonian stool (plate 21), supported by carved men and leopards, which was used mainly as a stand for a fruit-bowl and for the flowers that my father always brought with him when he visited. There was also the graceful pencil drawing in blue and white by Modigliani (now in the Garman Ryan Collection; plate 6) for a sculpture of a caryatid, as well as another pencil drawing, an illustration of Baudelaire's *Les Fleurs du Mal* (plate 23), one of his most poignant works; also the paintings of my sister Esther (fig. 3) and our brother Theodore (fig. 4) by my mother's Jewish artist-friend Fritz Mühsam, one of many refugees, either Dutch or German, who lived in a complex of studios close by. The portrait of Esther captures wonderfully her oriental-seeming, peach-like perfection and dark chestnut hair with reddish lights. Theodore (Theo) resembled her in his features and colouring except for his very black hair. I was more like my father, with wildly curling, intractable curls (fig. 5). It was in this room in the King's Road that I sat for the brooding, nearly life-size pencil drawing of myself aged eight which is now in the collection, too (plate 84).

The whole atmosphere was of high Bohemia. There was only one key to the house on a perilous string which hung inside the letterbox. Student friends, old

Fig. 2
Oakeswell Hall, the Garman
family home in Wednesbury

musicians and young artists from the nearby studio would simply fish for the key and walk in. (But no one was allowed in when my father came between 6 pm and 7 pm to visit my mother.) He sometimes took us all out to the Isolabella restaurant or to the Ballets Russes de Monte Carlo and to Sadlers Wells. Other painters came, certainly Matthew Smith, who was my father's oldest friend, later to be guest of honour at Wynne (Godley's) and my wedding. He gave many paintings to my father, some of which were later sold, but the glowing little flower piece by him (plate 70) is still in the collection.

My dear cousin Michael Wishart, whose lyrical *Moths on a Blue Path* (plate 34) is part of the Walsall collection, has described all this time far better than I can In his vivid but somewhat apocryphal autobiography, *High Diver*. He exactly sets the tone, roller skating down the King's Road to meet his little sweetheart Esther in the 1930s before the trendy Chelsea of boutiques appeared in the 'sixties.

Many of my father's portrait busts were arranged in this double room. I cannot remember them all except that, when I was younger, I was frightened of them, they were so lifelike – were they men and women or creatures made of another substance?

Later on, when my mother moved to Hyde Park Gate and became Lady Epstein, this house in Chelsea became Theo's home. He had a studio in what had been a potting-shed in the garden at the back, before his fatal illness and early death.

My mother liked to buy from friends, who are scarcely known, just because she loved their work – for instance Margaret Cardew, the talented sister of my Godmother Amy Stokes, or from Clive Gardiner, a professor from Goldsmiths College whose drawings and watercolours are represented in the collection.

To my great pleasure, my mother introduced me to the work Filippo de Pisis, who has become my favourite Post-Impressionist painter. She owned one of them:

a vibrant single apple which hung in her house in Italy. I do not know how she acquired the two admirable de Pisis for Walsall, as Italians are so proud of him and want to keep all his paintings in their country – he was a contemporary and friend of De Chirico and is now almost unknown outside his own country.

I should say some words about my mother's friend and co-collector, Sally Ryan, whom I met only briefly after the War when my mother had become Lady Epstein and I was living at Hyde Park Gate. Sally was very thin and always elegant (fig. 6), though suffering from advanced cancer of the throat, which prevented her from speaking. But, nothing deterred, she and my mother went on expeditions to country sales, looking together for prints, drawings and paintings. They both had flair and diverse tastes – and Sally had the generosity always to have a car at my mother's disposal as she had never learned to drive. My father would say to her, "Kathleen, if you were to learn to drive, I know your whole face would change." She did indeed have a very idiosyncratic expression, being both uplifted and abstracted at the same time, as though she were far away in a world of her own.

I think my mother only *really* began to collect with Sally after my father's death, although she had hunted far and wide for good things for the 'Little Gallery' in Kensington which she owned and ran as a hobby. Perhaps she was inspired by my father's love of collecting; perhaps she was sorry that much of his collection had gone and wanted to make reparation with her own collection.

I must also add to my list of familial paintings the portrait of myself against a shuttered window in Villefranche-sur-Mer (plate 51), done shortly after the birth of my eldest child, Anne, by my first husband, Lucian Freud, who also painted the watercolour portraits of Annie and Annabel, my second daughter, which are in Walsall together with his small oil painting of Kingcups.

Another familial work is a fine portrait in bronze of my Uncle Douglas Garman – my mother's eldest brother – by my cousin-in-law William Chattaway, who lives

FAR LEFT Fig. 3
Fritz Mühsam, *Esther*, oil on canvas, 46 × 38.5 cm (18⅛ × 15¼ in.), GR.174

LEFT Fig. 4
Fritz Mühsam, *Theo*, oil on canvas, 41.5 × 33.5 cm (16⅜ × 13¼ in.), GR.175

and works in France. Annie and Annabel are again portrayed in bronze as babies by my father (plate 82). They were subsequently arranged as a group by my mother as *The Sisters*, although they were made separately with four years' space between. And of course there are the very large paintings and pastels by Theodore, my brother – some made in London in my mother's room and others in South Harting, where he worked as a cowman (he was a conscientious objector during the War) in West Sussex close to my grandmother's house. I believe his painting of my grandmother's small but flower-crammed garden is the most popular in the entire collection (plate 28).

Theodore could only, at that time, paint at weekends, mainly the beechwoods and scenes of village life. Later on, after the War, he painted the contents of his house in Chelsea – not only some of the statues and carvings by his father, but the views from the windows and the stuff of daily life: the enamel coffee-pot with the rose, bought in the south of France; the kitchen sink; and the ancient gas oven. This was kitchen-sink painting long before John Bratby. His exuberant paintings have sadly not been enough recognized, especially his early pastels of the Black Country around Walsall Wood, where we often stayed with my mother's old nanny, Ada Newbould, for rather bleak holidays in her little house with a druggist's shop which belonged to her blind husband; Theo at this time was only sixteen years old! He captured wonderfully well the dereliction and sadness of the barren countryside with its slag heaps and decaying industrial machinery.

I like to think that my mother and Sally Ryan would be both surprised and pleased to know about The New Art Gallery built around their collection: my mother for Theodore's sake, Sally for that of her mentor and inspiration, and my father himself who, by his genius, was the original initiator of it all.

"I feel we are dealing with dreams . . .": The Story of the Garman Ryan Collection

Sheila McGregor

The appeal of the Garman Ryan Collection lies in its idiosyncrasy, its intriguing juxtapositions, the domestic scale of its contents and, above all, the almost palpable presence of the personalities whose lives influenced its creation. It is quite unlike any other public art collection in Great Britain.

Behind most public art collections of a distinctive character there lies a powerful individual, whether it be a wealthy entrepreneur collecting for reasons of pleasure, philanthropy or self-aggrandisement or a curator bringing her or his own personal interests and obsessions to bear on the business of developing a collection. In the Midlands alone there are examples of all the above: one thinks of Hans Hess, Assistant Keeper of Art in Leicester, using his personal connections with Weimar Germany to build up a collection of German Expressionist painting and prints in the 1940s; of curator David Rodgers defying municipal taste in Wolverhampton to create a strong collection of Pop art in the 1970s; of Sir William Barber setting out to rival the National Gallery in London with the collection of European 'masterpieces' now housed in The Barber Institute of Fine Arts at the University of Birmingham; of Whitworth Wallis, Birmingham Museum and Art Gallery's first curator, laying the foundations of what would become an outstanding Pre-Raphaelite collection.

The Garman Ryan Collection, however, strikes a very different note. It is unusual because it has no single thematic or art-historical focus; nor does it consist solely of what could be perceived as 'major' works, acquired with reference to a dominant canon. Instead, it embraces work from many different periods and cultures, giving equal weight to the famous and the little known. It tends to favour what might be described as 'work in progress', those aspects of an artist's output which provide insight into *process* rather than finished product. It celebrates and commemorates the friends and relations whose lives were intimately linked with those of the collection's founders. Most striking of all, this is a collection formed by two women working closely in partnership, at a time when collecting was still, predominantly, a male prerogative. When news of the potential gift of the Garman Ryan Collection to Walsall first broke in the local press in 1972, it was widely assumed that the benefactor must be a man.

Kathleen Garman (1901–1979)

In reality, the anonymous benefactor was Lady Kathleen Epstein, née Garman

(fig. 7), who had grown up in nearby Wednesbury. Her grandfather, a doctor, had moved there in the mid nineteenth century and her father, Walter Garman, had become the borough's progressive first Medical Officer of Health in 1884. Kathleen and her eight brothers and sisters spent their childhood at Oakeswell Hall, a well-known but much 'improved' medieval manor house in Wednesbury, which both served as the family home and provided space, in a separate building in the grounds, for her father's surgery.

The story of the Garman brothers and sisters (fig. 8) is a remarkable one, for almost all were to become involved with the more radical literary, artistic and political circles of British life between the wars. Kathleen's elder sister, Mary, entered into a volatile marriage with the South African poet Roy Campbell, which endured with turbulent interludes (including Mary's well-documented affair with Vita Sackville West) until Campbell's death in a car crash in 1957. Douglas became Education Secretary of the British Communist Party as a young man, and also worked as Assistant Editor of the important literary monthly *The Calendar of Modern Letters*. For a time in the 1930s he was romantically involved with the American art patron and collector Peggy Guggenheim. Mavin actively supported the Republican cause in the Spanish Civil War and spent many years as a rancher in Brazil, before eventually returning to Britain in later life. Helen married a local fisherman in the artists' colony of Martigues in southern France; later, after the death of her husband, she returned to London with her children and worked for the Free French during the Second World War. Her daughter Cathy married the writer Laurie Lee. Sylvia became the close friend of T.E. Lawrence, better known to the general public as Lawrence of Arabia. Lorna, the youngest of the family, married the publisher Ernest Wishart. Their son, Michael, became a successful painter, whose picture *Moths on a Blue Path* (plate 34) is represented in the Garman Ryan Collection.

It was with Mary Garman that Kathleen left home to study music in London in

ABOVE LEFT Fig. 7
Kathleen Garman
in 1921

ABOVE RIGHT Fig. 8
The Garman brothers and sisters (with Kathleen standing on the far left)

OPPOSITE Fig. 9
Jacob Epstein, *First Portrait of Kathleen*, 1921, bronze, height 47 cm (18 in.), GR.88

Fig. 10
Jacob Epstein, *Sally Ryan*,
1937, bronze, height 39 cm
(15 3/8 in.), GR.354

1917. There, in 1921, she met the sculptor Jacob Epstein and began a relationship which ended only with Epstein's death in 1959. Although Epstein was married and already a figure of some notoriety, Kathleen's devotion to him was absolute: she set up an alternative, parallel household to the 'official' one and had three children by Epstein in the years that followed – Theodore (known as Theo) in 1924, Kitty in 1926 and Esther in 1929.

With three children to support and no secure source of income, life for Kathleen cannot have been easy. Her loyalty to Epstein was severely tested by the hostility of his first wife, Margaret Dunlop, and by his subsequent liaison with Isobel Nicholas, by whom he had a son, Jackie, in 1934. Through it all, however, Kathleen's commitment to Epstein remained steadfast. When, after many years of illness, Margaret Dunlop died in 1947, Kathleen moved into his house at 18 Hyde Park Gate, London, bringing considerable organizational flair to the administration of the sculptor's affairs and the promotion of his work. Epstein and Kathleen eventually married in 1955, something Epstein had apparently wanted for many years. Perhaps their decision to marry was a symbolic reaffirmation of love in the face of recent bereavement, both Theo and Esther having died in tragic circumstances the year before.

Epstein's portrait bust of Kathleen (fig. 9), which was executed in the very early stages of their relationship and is the first of seven such portraits, reveals clearly the physical and intellectual qualities which first attracted him to her. She is remembered by all who knew her as a strikingly beautiful woman, whose charm, fortitude and somewhat awesome energy commanded respect and, often, extreme devotion in her friends. One such friend was the American sculptor Sally Ryan, whose likeness Epstein captured in a portrait bust of 1937 (fig. 10) and with whom Kathleen was later to create the Garman Ryan Collection.

Sally Ryan (1916–1968)

Kathleen's friendship with Sally Ryan began in 1935, when Sally, a promising young sculptor in her own right, introduced herself to Epstein. Sarah Tack Ryan, to give Sally her full name, was the granddaughter of Thomas Fortune Ryan, a highly successful Irish-American entrepreneur, whose business interests in shipping, railroads, insurance, gold, iron, rubber and tobacco enabled him to amass one of the largest fortunes in the United States. One less-than-flattering contemporary description characterized him as ". . . the most adroit, suave and noiseless man in American finance".[1]

Thomas Fortune Ryan was also a patron of the visual arts. In 1909 he commissioned a portrait bust of himself from Rodin (now in the Tate Gallery, London) and subsequently donated several works by Rodin to the Metropolitan Museum of Art in New York. His personal art collection encompassed paintings, rare books and prints, enamels, oriental carpets, Italian majolica, Renaissance furniture and Italian Renaissance sculpture, all of which the young Sally must have known and from which she must have drawn some inspiration. Probably even more influential, though, was Thomas Fortune Ryan's relationship with his lawyer John Quinn, the first and most important of Epstein's patrons, who had purchased some of the artist's most notable carvings and provided crucial financial support in the precarious early stages of his career. It may well have been through Quinn that Sally first encountered Epstein's work.[2]

Thus Sally's family background provided every encouragement to follow an artistic career. There was, in addition, an auspicious family precedent in the person of her uncle, Augustus Vincent Tack (from whom Sally inherited her middle name), who was one of the most prominent painters of the day. His vast, mystical, semi-abstract landscapes, many of which can be seen in the Phillips Collection in Washington, D.C., had a seminal impact on the more famous generation of American abstract painters (Jackson Pollock, Mark Rothko, Clyfford Still *et al.*) which emerged in the 1940s and 1950s.

Sally's own career began in Canada, where she had spent much of her childhood. At the age of only sixteen, in 1933, she exhibited her first sculpture at the Royal Canadian Academy of Arts in Toronto and the following year went to study with the sculptor Jean Camus in Paris, where she achieved an 'honourable mention' at the annual Salon with the arresting portrait of a Martinique woman (fig. 12) now in the Garman Ryan Collection. She showed this work at the Royal Academy of Arts, London, in 1935, the year in which she also met Epstein for the first time. From then on, her work would often be compared with his. A review of her exhibition in 1937 at the Marie Sterner Galleries in New York presents her more or less explicitly as Epstein's disciple:

> . . . her talent is considerable, and it runs along the lines favoured by Epstein
> himself in his portrait bronzes. They have the same deft modelling and the

OPPOSITE Fig. 11
Sally Ryan with the armature
of a sculpture

RIGHT Fig. 12
Sally Ryan, *The Martinique*,
1934, bronze, height 31 cm
(12 in.), GR.224

FAR RIGHT Fig. 13
Sally Ryan at work on a
sculpture in the mid-1940s

same somewhat adventitious emphasis on rough surfaces to secure the semblance of power. This is, to be sure, not 'original seeing' so much as seeing through the eyes of Epstein and even of Rodin in his more emotional figures.[3]

Her choice of subject-matter and vigorous portrait style are indeed very close to Epstein's. But what little evidence remains of her sculpture suggests some interesting differences, too, and her later flower paintings have a quiet intensity which is very far removed from Epstein's more flamboyant style.

Described by friends and family members as "shy", "private" and "basically never adjusted to the run of the world", Sally remains an elusive figure. Those relatives who remember her have speculated that her parents' painful and highly public divorce in the 1920s may account, at least in part, for her apparent aloofness. At a time when same-sex relationships were far less tolerated than they are now, Sally was doubtless also reluctant to publicize the fact that she lived with another woman, Ellen Ballon, who was later the chief beneficiary of her will.

A newspaper feature which accompanied her exhibition at the Wildenstein Galleries in New York in 1944 offers a typically journalistic but nonetheless revealing portrait of Sally as a young woman:

> You'd never think, to look at sculptor Sally Ryan, that she was born to millions. The granddaughter of the late Thomas Fortune Ryan, who piled up a fortune in Wall Street, spends most of her time in sweater and slacks, applying chisel to marble – a pair of horn-rimmed spectacles on her nose, a pair of battered oxfords on her feet. One of them is slit across the front and has a way of gaping open in the most embarrassing way. This causes Sally to redden, clap her hand over the slit and say in an agonized undertone, "I hoped that wouldn't happen while you were here."

Jacob Epstein

Her friends will tell you that Sally owns some very snappy clothes, and that she is a knock-out when she has them on. The only trouble is to get her to put them on. She has a way of falling in love with one old coat and wearing it till it's almost shiny on the seams or till one of her friends says "For heaven's sake! Sally, go get yourself some clothes."

Sally, who says she is 27, is sandy-haired, blue-eyed, fair-skinned and frail. She is the daughter of Allan A. Ryan and one of a large family who inherited the Ryan fortune . . .[4]

The fortune to which this article refers enabled Sally to pursue her career free from the usual financial pressures (fig. 13). But she was apparently conscious of the need to employ her money usefully, and when, in the late 1950s, she discovered that she was terminally ill with cancer of the throat, she decided to channel some of her personal fortune into the creation of the collection which eventually came to Walsall, *via* Kathleen Epstein, in 1973.

Jacob Epstein (1880–1959)

It was through Epstein that Kathleen and Sally first met and it is Epstein whose life and work dominate their collection. His friendships and his aesthetic and intellectual interests are ever present, providing a leitmotif which unites what would otherwise seem, at first sight, an extremely miscellaneous collection. Through the many works by Epstein in the Garman Ryan Collection (in fact the largest single holding of his work anywhere), it is possible to trace the career of one of the century's great sculptors, to chart the obsessions, innovations and controversies which set him apart from his contemporaries and made it possible for other pioneering sculptors to follow in his wake. As Henry Moore would later acknowledge, "He took the brickbats, he took the insults, he faced the howls of derision . . . and as far as sculpture in this century is concerned, he took them first."[5]

Epstein was born in 1880, the child of first-generation Jewish–Polish immigrants living in the heart of New York City's Jewish community on the Lower East Side and the second of eight brothers and sisters. From early childhood he drew continually, apparently never in any doubt about his vocation as an artist. His few surviving early drawings include *Lunch in the Shop* (fig. 14), a sympathetic depiction of immigrant workers taking a break from the drudgery of the sweatshop. It was with drawings such as this that Epstein first achieved success: in 1901 he was commissioned to provide illustrations for a book by the journalist Hutchins Hapgood entitled *The Spirit of the Ghetto*, a vivid account of Jewish life in the New York ghetto at a critical moment of cultural transition, as age-old traditions and customs merged with those of a newer, faster-moving society.

With the money he had earned from Hapgood's commission, Epstein set off for Paris, determined to consolidate his studies and his reputation. His self-portrait

of 1901 (fig. 15) conveys an impression of rebelliousness, even arrogance, which was probably not too far from the truth. In Paris, Epstein studied at the Ecole des Beaux-Arts and the Académie Julian and drew regular inspiration from the city's great ethnographic collections – although it would be some time yet before these experiences found formal expression in his work. Already he was making sculpture, albeit in a conventional, naturalistic style: the tenderly observed *Baby Awake* (fig. 16) and related drawings date from his time in Paris between 1902 and 1904.

In 1905 Epstein moved to London, armed with an introductory letter from Rodin, whom he had met in Paris and much admired. For Epstein, the urge to realise his ideas in three-dimensional form was by now irresistible. He found he could derive greater physical and mental satisfaction from the process of making sculpture than drawing on its own had ever been able to provide. His energies were now fixed on carving, something he had experimented with, unsuccessfully, in Paris, but was determined to master.

The pre-eminence of carving over modelling was to become a fundamental tenet of the modernist creed. But at the turn of the century, carving was firmly out of fashion, and the idea of 'direct carving' (the practice of working direct on the stone, without recourse to preliminary models or to mechanical measuring devices) was regarded in academic circles as crude and regressive. To Epstein, however, the possibilities offered by a direct physical engagement with his materials were enormous: it was a way of making sculpture which promised a new and invigorating expressiveness, with the power to communicate elemental truths about human experience.

In 1907 the invitation from the architect Charles Holden to make a series of sculptures for the new British Medical Association building (now Zimbabwe House) on the Strand, London, opposite Charing Cross Station, provided Epstein with his

first major public commission and a first opportunity to make carvings on a grand scale (fig. 17). He rose to the occasion with a series of eighteen sculptures which portray the seven ages of man, as well as figures symbolizing Medicine, Health and Chemical Research. It was, perhaps surprisingly, the gentle and dignified figure of *Maternity* (plate 19), a semi-naked, pregnant woman, which provoked the media furore that suddenly engulfed Epstein in 1908 and precipitated him from relative obscurity into a glare of hostile publicity. This, proclaimed *The London Evening Standard*, was "a form of statuary which no careful father would wish his daughter, or no discriminating young man his fiancé to see."[6] Although Epstein had many eminent supporters, the controversy ensured that everything he subsequently undertook would be scrutinized and debated in a spirit of moral censure.

The tomb of Oscar Wilde (fig. 18), for which there is a preparatory drawing in the collection (plate 18), was yet another collaboration with Charles Holden and, perhaps more predictably in this case, the focus of a second major scandal. The mere fact of commemorating the life and work of a writer notorious for his homosexuality was enough to excite the critics; but when Epstein's sculpture, a massive

Fig. 18
Jacob Epstein, tomb of Oscar
Wilde, Père Lachaise
Cemetery, Paris, 1909–12

sphinx-like angel, was eventually unveiled in Père Lachaise Cemetery in Paris in 1912, the authorities took exception to its prominent genitalia and decreed that they must either be removed or covered.

Throughout the pre-war years, Epstein experimented continually with carving, exploring themes – sexual and maternal love, fertility, procreation, birth – which departed radically from sculptural convention. His formal vocabulary, too, entailed a break with the classical European past. In common with other artists of the avantgarde, he was now obsessively interested in the art of African, Asian, South American and Oceanic cultures, finding in what was then classed as 'aboriginal' sculpture a vitality, sensitivity to materials and formal inventiveness which suited his own creative purposes.

At about this time, Epstein began to assemble what would develop into one of the largest and most distinguished private collections of so-called 'primitive' art in the world, a collection which grew over the years to approximately one thousand items and came to fill every corner of his London home (fig. 19). He lavished large amounts of money on his collection, often at moments when he could ill afford the expense. His pursuit of the objects on which he had set his sights was single-minded and he was never in any doubt about the accuracy of his own aesthetic judgement. The *Mask of Nefertiti* (plate 55) in the Garman Ryan Collection is possi-

Fig. 19
View of Epstein's home at
18 Hyde Park Gate, London,
ca. 1959

bly a copy, but Epstein was convinced not only of its authenticity but also of its superiority over the famous version now in Berlin.

In the light of recent debates about the essentially colonial nature of Western artists' preoccupation with the art of other cultures, it would be easy to dismiss Epstein's collecting as exploitative – a symptom and product of unequal power relations between Europe and the rest of the world. But although his understanding of iconographic context was sometimes limited, he felt a strong sense of kinship with the unknown tribal sculptors whose art he admired, he recognized the individual qualities of their work and he marvelled at the sheer variety of ways in which they represented the human form.

Preparatory drawings for Epstein's sculpture show him appropriating from a wide range of cultural sources and reveal a complex process of assimilation and synthesis, which would often result in something far removed from the prototype. His many drawings for *Rock Drill* (plate 22), for example, underwent a long evolution, from a series of initial studies on paper which refer explicitly to African sculpture to the drawing in the Garman Ryan Collection, which comes close to the sculptor's final conception.

First exhibited at the London Group exhibition in March 1915, *Rock Drill* (fig. 20) was Epstein's most famous sculpture, a vast and menacing assemblage

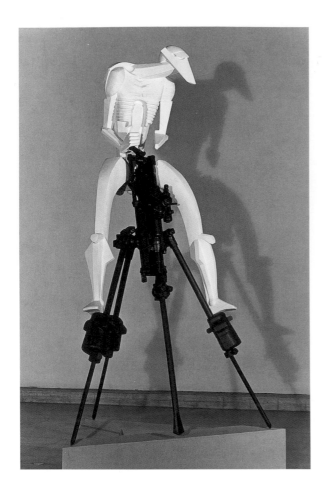

which shows man locked in ambiguous alliance with machine, at once the instigator of destructive violence and its pathetic victim. It consisted, in Epstein's own words, of ". . . a machine-like robot, visored, menacing and carrying within itself its progeny, protectively ensconced", and it incorporated – at the time its most astonishing feature – a real mechanical drill.[7] Writing with the benefit of hindsight, the sculptor later presented it as a conscious symbolization of the death and destruction unleashed by the First World War.

At the time of its creation, however, Epstein's intentions were less clearly anti-war. *Rock Drill* was made at the height of his association with the short-lived Vorticist movement, the only grouping of British artists in the pre-war period to advocate an art of almost total abstraction. Led by the arch-propagandist Wyndham Lewis, the Vorticists responded to the increasing speed and mechanization of modern life with the use of aggressively abstract and geometric imagery. In 1915 *Rock Drill* was seen by many commentators as the ultimate embodiment of this radical and essentially optimistic machine aesthetic.

But for Epstein, in common with other artists, the First World War was a watershed. He lost such close friends as the sculptor Gaudier-Brzeska and the philosopher T.E. Hulme, and he himself suffered a nervous breakdown following a long and unsuccessful campaign to be recruited as a war artist. It seems likely that both his Jewishness and his controversial public image predisposed the authorities against him.

Artistically, Epstein became convinced of the need to change direction, for abstraction no longer seemed adequate to the task of dealing with the legacy of war: "I never saw the abstract as an end in itself", he later said, "and I do not agree with people who would divorce art entirely from human interest. They argue amongst other things that the possibilities of pure form are endless. That is not the case. They are limited like patterns in a children's kaleidoscope."[8]

The impulse both to simplify and to exaggerate aspects of the human form remained strong. Epstein continued to borrow heavily from non-European traditions, especially in such large-scale carvings as *Genesis* (1930), *Behold the Man (Ecce Homo)* (1934–35), *Adam* (1938–39) and *Jacob and the Angel* (1939–40), and in the public commissions which still, from time to time, came his way. But the general trend of Epstein's work in the period between the wars is towards a calmer, more humanistic vision of his fellow men, a vision characterized by dignity, humour and psychological insight.

Significantly, his first major full-length figure in the later stages of the War was the *Risen Christ* (1917–19; fig. 21), whose majestic, upright stance powerfully embodies the idea of resurrection, while at the same time transmitting through the dramatic gesture of the hands (fig. 22) a stern reminder of human failing. Critics were quick to react against Epstein's refusal of comforting stereotype (the head was a naturalistic portrait of his friend Bernard van Dieren) and many questioned the legitimacy of a Jew representing the figure of Christ at all – thus initiating the strain of anti-Semitic criticism which disfigured discussion of his work between the wars. To the critics, his *Madonna and Child* of 1926, a smaller version of which can be seen in the Garman Ryan Collection (fig. 23), was further proof of an alien

BELOW LEFT Fig. 22
Jacob Epstein, *Hands of the Risen Christ*, 1917–19, bronze, height 31 cm (12 in.), GR.90

BELOW RIGHT Fig. 23
Jacob Epstein, *Heads of the New York Madonna and Child*, ca 1926–27, bronze, height 48.2 cm (19 in.), GR.362

mentality ill-suited to the interpretation of New Testament themes, for the models were clearly of Asian rather than European appearance.

The features of the *Madonna and Child* were based on an Indian woman called Amina Peerbhoy (otherwise known as Sunita) and her son Enver, whom Epstein had met in 1924 and who were at that time living in his house at Guilford Street in Bloomsbury. Under the watchful but accommodating eye of the first Mrs Epstein, the sculptor maintained an open house, providing food and lodgings for a succession of friends and acolytes: the 'gypsy' woman Nan Condron, who also acted as household maid, Sunita and Enver, and the model known as Dolores were all, at different times, adopted by the Epsteins.

Other friendships played a still more significant part in the artist's life. In 1916 he met the actress Meum Lindsell-Stewart (plate 54), who moved into his house and became, in 1918, the mother of his first child, Peggy Jean. After Meum's departure from the scene, Peggy Jean was raised by Margaret, Epstein's wife, as her own daughter. The sculptor's affair with Kathleen Garman in 1921 and the arrival of a second unofficial family further complicated his domestic affairs. The fact that he was often seen in public with Kathleen (fig. 24) and made no secret of their attachment doubtless served to reinforce his reputation as a man who lived outside the norms of respectable society.

During the 1920s Epstein was never long out of the public eye. He was commissioned in 1922 to create a memorial in Hyde Park to the writer and naturalist W.H. Hudson and chose as his theme the female spirit Rima from Hudson's novel *Green Mansions*. Once again, the extreme stylization of Epstein's approach raised a hue and cry and the by now predictable accusation that his work was somehow 'un-English' in spirit. His relief carvings of *Day* and *Night* for the new London Underground Headquarters in 1928 were attacked for similar reasons. In the popular press Epstein had come to epitomize all that was considered degenerate about 'modern art'.

Yet Epstein was also, paradoxically, finding considerable success as a portrait sculptor. Rabindranath Tagore, the great Indian poet and writer (fig. 25 and plate 53), was one of his most eminent sitters during this period; other commissions included Joseph Conrad, Ramsay Macdonald, Paul Robeson, Albert Einstein and George Bernard Shaw. In some quarters, at least, public taste had moved on: the roughness of surface treatment, which might at one time have been perceived as lack of finesse, was now understood and admired as the very thing which gave Epstein's portraits their impression of life. He himself had come to regard modelling as the more truly creative of the two conventional approaches to making sculpture:

> It is the creating of something out of nothing. An actual building up and getting to grips with material. In carving the suggestion for the form of the work often comes from the shape of the block. In fact inspiration is always modified by the material, there is no complete freedom, while in modelling

Fig. 24
Epstein and Kathleen Garman visiting the W.H. Hudson Memorial, Hyde Park, London, from *The Sphere*, 30 May 1925

Fig. 25
Epstein with Rabindranath
Tagore, 1926

the artist is entirely unfettered by anything save the technical difficulties of his own chosen subject. As I see sculpture it must not be rigid. It must quiver with life, while carving often leads a man to neglect the flow and rhythm of life.[2]

With his portraits, Epstein at last achieved positive recognition and some commercial success. But it was only through painting and illustration that he could guarantee a steady income. At intervals throughout the 1920s and 1930s, Epstein spent time living and working in a rented house in Loughton, on the edge of Epping Forest. The vibrant gouache *Autumn Landscape, Epping Forest* (plate 29) is one of nearly a hundred paintings he made of the forest during a stay there in 1933, while his painting of *Sunflowers* (plate 68) belongs to a series of flower studies made in 1943, initially in response to a commission from a firm of Dutch art dealers. What had begun as a commercial proposition rapidly developed into an obsession, and, for a time, he abandoned sculpture entirely in order to explore this new and unexpected source of inspiration. According to his son Jackie, Epstein went as far as to employ a gardener in order to ensure a generous supply of flowers for his painting. His first love, book illustration, could also prove a profitable and absorbing pastime: with a dramatic series of Old Testament drawings and commissions such as the one to illustrate Baudelaire's *Les Fleurs du Mal* in 1936 (plate 23), Epstein found a useful means of supplementing his income, even if the critics continued to complain about his allegedly sensationalist approach to familiar subject-matter.

The later stages of Epstein's career were a good deal less controversial than his early years. In part, this was a consequence of changing fashion. Other younger artists such as Henry Moore and Barbara Hepworth were now stealing the critical limelight with works which, at their most extreme, had divested themselves almost entirely of figurative content. To Epstein, by contrast, an art that did not concern itself manifestly with the human figure and the mysteries of human motivation was unthinkable. The fact is, too, that the religious themes which interested him were not in tune with the increasingly secular mood of the times. Between 1929 and 1949 he was given no opportunity to create a large-scale public work of art.

In the commemorative climate of the post-war period, however, Epstein found his talents once more in demand. Several public commissions, almost all of a religious nature, followed the Second World War, among them the Cavendish Square *Madonna and Child* (1950–52), *Christ in Majesty* for Llandaff Cathedral (1954–55), the *TUC War Memorial* (1956–57) and the figure of *St Michael and the Devil* for Coventry Cathedral (1956–58). Alongside such major commissions, Epstein continued to undertake portraits, being by now sufficiently respected and senior an artist to be trusted with the responsibility of portraying the nation's most prominent public figures. An impressive list of sitters included individuals as diverse as Winston Churchill, Ernest Bevan, Pandit Nehru, Otto Klemperer, T.S. Eliot and Princess Margaret. Epstein's knighthood in 1954 confirmed, in the most public and prestigious of ways, his status as a pioneer of modern sculpture and elder statesman of British art. Although the last few years of his life were marked by tragedy, he at least had the satisfaction of knowing that the importance of his contribution to the development of British sculpture in the twentieth century had at long last been understood and acknowledged by the Establishment against which he had struggled for so long.

The Garman Ryan Collection

Precisely why and when Kathleen Garman conceived the idea of making her own art collection is hard to establish. After Epstein's death, in accordance with the provisions of his will, she sold off his collection of tribal and classical sculpture and artefacts, retaining only a few of the items which had held a special significance for her husband: for example, the Egyptian plaster mask of *Queen Nefertiti* (plate 55), a *Maori Greenstone Tiki* (plate 17) and a Roman marble *Head of a Mourning Woman* (plate 4). Over three hundred objects were sold to the private collector Carlo Monzino, while others found their way into some of the world's most famous museum collections, including the British Museum and the Metropolitan Museum of Art in New York.

Epstein had apparently sanctioned the sale out of concern for Kathleen's material well-being after his death. There were also issues of space to consider, for

the rambling house they had shared in Hyde Park Gate was much too big for Kathleen on her own. Yet it seems curious, even so, that Kathleen began so soon to collect in a similar vein. It may be that on some deep, psychological level she felt the need to start afresh, to create a collection that was truly hers. Having lived for so long in the shadow of a celebrated artist, she perhaps relished the opportunity to demonstrate her own creativity and aesthetic acumen.

At what juncture Sally and Kathleen joined forces remains unclear. Sally had purchased Epstein's *Madonna and Child* in 1938 and the remarkable early *Sun God Relief* in 1950 (on the reverse of which Epstein had carved *Primeval Gods* during 1931–33; fig. 26). By the time of Epstein's death, she knew that her own life expectancy was limited and was already planning for the future. In 1957 she wrote to the vicar of the Riverside Church in New York, "Because the interdenominational unity of Riverside Church is the nearest in expression that I have yet found to my personal belief, it would give me great comfort to feel that after my death a simple Protestant service could be held there . . . If this could be, for the sake of my

Fig. 27
Kathleen Garman as collector
and dealer, mid-1960s

friends, it would give me now great peace of mind."[10] It was to the Riverside Church that she gave Epstein's *Madonna and Child* in 1960, shortly after his death. The *Sun God Relief* she later bequeathed to the Metropolitan Museum of Art in the sculptor's memory.

For Sally, the idea of forming a collection with Epstein's widow, Kathleen Garman, would have seemed a natural consolidation of her links with the family. But it is difficult to ascertain exactly when their collaboration began and, more importantly, just how purposeful it was. Were purchases always considered jointly, for instance? And did the two women collect with agreed criteria in mind? A brief note from Sally to Kathleen informing her about the purchase of Bonnard's *The River Seine at Vernon* reads, "Dearest Kathy, This BONNARD landscape 'La Seine à Vernon' is for you, with my love – Sally. Easter 1966."[11] The informality of Sally's tone suggests that this was, at least at times, a collection which grew with a degree of spontaneity and that each was sufficiently confident of the other's taste to tolerate independent decision-making. On many other occasions, however, they clearly went 'shopping' together, and by the mid 1960s Kathleen was explicitly referring to her collection as the "Garman Ryan". But if the name of the collection had by now been settled, its contents were by no means fixed. There is evidence among Kathleen's papers of numerous acquisitions that did not, in the end, find a permanent home in the collection which came to Walsall in 1973.

The picture is further complicated by the fact that Kathleen ran her own commercial gallery after Epstein's death and was therefore buying and selling work on a regular basis (fig. 27). The 'Little Gallery', as it was known, operated from premises at 5 Kensington Church Walk from the mid 1960s, under the auspices of Kathleen's close friend Beth Lipkin. Many of the gallery's exhibitions took as their starting-point the themes (childhood, animals *etc*) which later furnished a framework for the display of the Garman Ryan Collection, and some of the works now in the collection are by such artists as Alice Weldon, Ian Seymour Wells and Margaret Cardew, who showed at Kathleen's gallery. It is highly likely that several Garman Ryan pictures were originally 'Little Gallery' stock.

But however fortuitous the pattern of acquisition, there can be no doubting the consistency of the vision which guided Sally and Kathleen in their collecting. This is a collection formed by two women who understood the nature of creativity, in particular the importance of exploration and experimentation to the creative process. Sally was, after all, a practising artist; and Kathleen had spent her entire adult life in the company of an artist who was not only intensely productive himself but also keenly interested in the creativity of others. It is no accident that the collection contains an unusually high proportion of works on paper and that many of its prints and drawings reveal unexpected aspects of artists more famous for their rhetorical history and genre scenes. Landseer's *Study of Wayside Plants* or Delacroix's charcoal sketch of a *New Born Lamb* (plate 71) are only two of the most notable examples.

There is a certain social and cultural egalitarianism, too, about the Garman Ryan Collection. Not for Kathleen and Sally the usual apostolic succession of great male artists, their work arranged in predictable chronological sequence. Almost all the artists are men, it is true. But some of the greatest names in the lexicon of European art – Dürer, Rembrandt, Monet, Van Gogh, Degas – take their place on equal terms alongside unknown artists from other parts of the world. A surprising number of the images in the collection show people at work or engaged in leisure activities – the stuff of ordinary, everyday life. And the thematic arrangement on which Kathleen insisted invites the viewer to examine each work on its own merits, to consider the universality of the impulses which inspire human beings to make works of art. In the relativistic cultural climate of the 1990s, it is easy to forget just how novel this display philosophy must have seemed when the collection was first shown. The Garman Ryan Collection is, to borrow John Berger's phrase, a collection about "ways of seeing".

The Garman Ryan Collection is also full of references to family and friends. Important early friends such as Augustus John, Gaudier-Brzeska and Modigliani are

FAR LEFT Fig. 28
Epstein with his grand-
daughter Annabel Freud,
ca. 1952–53

LEFT Fig. 29
Epstein's granddaughter Anne
Freud with the sculptor's
dog, Frisky

represented, in the case of Modigliani by a singularly beautiful drawing of a caryatid (plate 6) which was given to Epstein by the artist in Paris in *ca.* 1912. Matthew
Smith, probably Epstein's closest and longest-standing friend, is represented by
two works (plate 70) – all that remain of the extensive collection of Smith's work
which Epstein was forced to sell in 1939 for financial reasons.

Family relationships are acknowledged in numerous works of, and sometimes
by, members of the Epstein/Garman clan. There is the penetrating portrait of
Epstein's daughter Kitty by her first husband, Lucian Freud (plate 51); two charm-
ing portraits by Epstein himself of Kitty's baby daughters, Anne and Annabel Freud
(see also figs. 28 and 29); a sculpted head of Douglas Garman by his son-in-law,
William Chattaway; and portrait busts of Epstein's daughters Kitty and Esther. (The
First Portrait of Esther (plate 81) Epstein regarded as the finest thing he had ever
done.) Frisky, Epstein's much-loved sheep-dog and his constant companion in old
age, makes an appearance too (plate 79). The annals of Epstein/Garman family
history abound with stories of Frisky's affectionate nature and intelligence, especially his skill at negotiating the perils of London traffic.

A still more poignant presence are Kathleen's children by Epstein, Esther and
Theo Garman (figs. 30 and 31). Theo, Kathleen's eldest son, inherited his father's
artistic ability, as well as his passion for collecting. There are no fewer than fifteen
works by Theo in the Garman Ryan Collection, several of which feature items from
his collection of medieval religious works of art. A French Gothic wood-carving of
Christ with Crown of Thorns, for instance, appears in the paintings *Good Friday* and
Window Picture in June (figs. 32 and 33). Colourful and crammed with incident,
Theo's paintings reflect his temperament: friends and relations remember him as a
warm and generous person, who well deserved his nickname 'Sunny'.

RIGHT Fig. 30
Esther Garman

FAR RIGHT Fig. 31
Theo and Esther Garman

Yet from at least the mid 1940s he was also subject to recurrent bouts of depression. He registered as a conscientious objector during the War and spent three years working as a farm labourer in South Harting, West Sussex, where Kathleen's mother had been living for many years in Vine Cottage – a haven for the Garman family throughout the 1930s and especially during the Blitz. In 1945, following a prolonged period of depression, Theo tried to take his own life and was admitted to hospital. Despite some recognition as a professional artist over the next few years, including a successful one-person exhibition at the Redfern Gallery in 1950 (for which Matthew Smith wrote the catalogue introduction), Theo's mental health declined. He died of a heart attack while being admitted to hospital in 1954, in circumstances which have never been fully clarified.

Only ten months later, the family suffered a further devastating loss: Esther, Kathleen's much-loved younger daughter, committed suicide. For some time, the centre of Esther's emotional life had been a close but complicated relationship with Mark Joffé, whose son, Roland, she looked after as her own child. But the immediate cause of her unhappiness was the death of her brother and the suicide of a young man whose offer of marriage she had rejected. On 13 November 1954 Epstein broke the news of Esther's death to his daughter Peggy Jean in America: "Esther who was so beautiful and well-loved by all committed suicide . . . At the moment one can think of nothing else and lives in a distracted and almost demented manner . . . I hope Kathleen will come out of it, in time." After Esther's funeral, he wrote again, "Things are still bad. Both Theo and Esther were buried in one grave in a quiet graveyard in Sussex where they were both brought up as children . . . I hope time will heal so much tragedy."[12]

For Kathleen, the creation of the Garman Ryan Collection was perhaps, in

OPPOSITE Fig. 32
Theo Garman, *Window
Picture in June*, oil on canvas,
183 × 122 cm
(72⅛ × 48⅛ in.), GR.107

RIGHT Fig. 33
Theo Garman at work on a
portrait. *Window Picture in
June* can be seen on the
right-hand wall

part, a means of coming to terms with her bereavement, its gift to Walsall twenty
years later in some sense an act of remembrance and reparation. Although
Kathleen spent much of her adult life in London, she had regularly returned to
Walsall to visit her nanny Ada Newbould, who fostered Esther for several years and
was always on hand to provide support during times of crisis. Ada's daughter,
Rosie, remembers Kathleen as a slightly "overwhelming" figure, but she looked
forward immensely to Kathleen's visits and has vivid memories of her own trips to
London to stay with Kathleen and her children. Rosie frequently sat for Theo (she
is the *Blue Girl* in his painting of that title) and fondly remembers their joint excur-
sions to Stubbers Green in Shelfield, at that time an unspoilt beauty spot which
inspired one of Theo's most vibrant sketches (plate 36).[13]

Thus, despite Kathleen's bohemian and metropolitan lifestyle, there was
never a time when she lost touch with her native Black Country. So when, after
Sally's death, she began to ponder the problem of where to house her collection,
she instinctively returned to her roots. It is said that in 1972 she was shown the
first-floor Reference Room of Walsall Library (which had been endowed, in 1906, by

Andrew Carnegie) and fell instantly in love with its graceful proportions and intricately moulded ceiling (fig. 34). With her mind now made up, she began negotiations with the borough council.

The Garman Ryan Collection eventually opened to the public on 9 July 1974. Correspondence relating to the gift reveals a good deal about Kathleen's aspirations for the collection. It represented the realisation of a dream, she said, ". . . the culmination of an idea I have been working for, for the last twelve years."[14] She felt sure, from the outset, that it would appeal to a wide audience. When, in October 1972, there was some talk of organizing a preview exhibition, she wrote to the then town clerk, "I think we are all agreed that we would want to put up the best possible show from every point of view. I would like it to be a model of its kind at the same time striking a note of intimacy and spontaneity that will appeal to all ages."[15] Kathleen also appreciated what her collection could do for a community which was otherwise sparsely endowed with leisure amenities of any kind. In May 1977 she wrote, "It seems to me from the start the collection has been run just as I would have wished – quietly, efficiently and courteously, providing local residents and many visitors from abroad with a little haven of peace and visual and intellectual interest. We have never made any pretentious claims, but I do believe the Collection has come to mean quite a lot to people round about."[16]

What Kathleen would have made of her collection's new home in The New Art Gallery one can only guess. But the care with which she attended to the practical detail of its original display (stressing the need for a cafeteria and vetting the selection of wall and carpet colour) suggests that she would have approved of the sensitivity which the architects and curatorial team have brought to the presentation of the Garman Ryan Collection in its new setting. She would certainly have applauded The New Art Gallery's emphasis on children, as would Epstein himself: a glance round the collection makes their love of children abundantly clear. She would surely have approved of the gallery's commitment to the support of new and sometimes controversial work, having shared her life with a sculptor whose ambitions were often frustrated by prejudice and lack of opportunity. And it seems likely, too, that she would have understood The New Art Gallery's potential to act as a catalyst for economic and educational renewal within the Borough of Walsall. "I feel we are dealing with dreams", she wrote in 1973, "and are about to house them in a solid Midlands setting for posterity. How delightful."[17] Little did she know then that the dream she had shared with Sally Ryan would enable others to dream too; that at the turn of the century Walsall would embark on the creation of a new purpose-built gallery with her gift, the Garman Ryan Collection, at its heart.

Notes

1. The remark is commonly attributed to Ryan's business partner, William C. Whitney.

2. Benjamin L. Reid, *The Man from New York: John Quinn and his Friends*, New York 1968, p. 84. I am grateful to Antonia Payne for drawing this source to my attention.

3. *World Telegraph*, 23 October 1937.

4. Unsourced press cutting, The Epstein Archive, Walsall.

5. Henry Moore's obituary notice for Epstein, *The Sunday Times*, 23 August 1959.

6. *The London Evening Standard*, 19 June 1908.

7. Jacob Epstein, *Let There Be Sculpture: An Autobiography*, London 1940, p. 70.

8. Arnold Haskell, *The Sculptor Speaks: Jacob Epstein to Arnold L. Haskell: A Series of Conversations on Art*, London 1931, p. 44.

9. *Ibid.*, p. 61.

10. Letter from Sally Ryan to Dr Robert J. McCracken, 2 August 1957. Quoted in Dr McCracken's address at Sally Ryan's memorial service, The Epstein Archive, Walsall.

11. On loan to The Epstein Archive, Walsall.

12. Letters from Epstein to Peggy Jean Epstein, 13 and 27 November 1954, Tate Gallery Archives.

13. Letter and statement from Rosie Price to Jo Digger, 1 December 1997.

14. Letter from Kathleen Garman to J.A. Galloway, 11 October 1972.

15. *Ibid.*

16. Letter from Kathleen Garman to John Morgan, 4 May 1977.

17. Letter from Kathleen Garman to Michael Mossesson, 3 December 1973.

Figure Studies

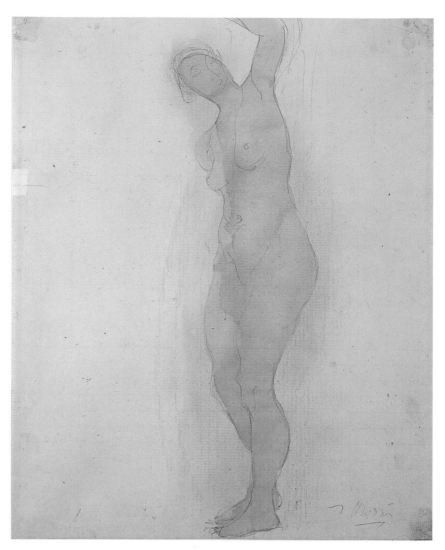

1. Auguste Rodin, *Nude Study*, watercolour and pencil, 27 × 21.5 cm (10⅝ × 8½ in.), GR.208

2. Francisco de Goya, *Grotesque Dance (Baile grotesco)*, from the 'Disparates/Proverbios' series, *ca.* 1819–20, etching, 25 × 36 cm (9⅞ × 14¼ in.), GR.131

3. Pierre Bonnard, Poster for *La Revue Blanche*, 1894,
lithograph poster, 76 × 58.5 cm (29⁷/₈ × 23¹/₈ in.), GR.355

4. Roman, *Head of a mourning woman*, 1st century AD, marble, height 30 cm (11⁷/₈ in.), GR.285

5. Edgar Degas, *Woman Washing her Left Leg (Femme se lavant sa jambe gauche)*, 1895, cast *ca.* 1919–21, bronze, height 14.5 cm (5³/₄ in.), GR.34

6. Amedeo Modigliani

Caryatid (Cariatide), *ca.* 1913–14,
pencil and blue crayon,
55 × 41.5 cm (21⁵/₈ × 16³/₈ in.), GR.170
ILLUSTRATED OPPOSITE

Modigliani is now most famous for his paintings, but his earlier ambition was to become a sculptor. The word 'caryatid' comes from the ancient Greek for a carved figure that acts as a pillar supporting the roof of a building. Modigliani made many drawings of caryatids as designs for an ambitious 'Temple of Beauty' dedicated to the glory of all humankind. His dream to build a 'new parthenon' was never realized and ill-health forced him to give up carving, leaving only one roughly shaped caryatid, now in the Museum of Modern Art, New York.

The Garman Ryan Collection's caryatid was drawn while Modigliani and Jacob Epstein were both working in Paris. They shared similar backgrounds, both being Jewish and having left their native countries in search of a bohemian life in Paris, and they had a common interest in direct carving and the architectural possibilities of sculpture. They became friends, and Modigliani gave this caryatid drawing to Epstein, who gave it pride of place in his collection. The influence of Picasso and African and Eastern Art can be seen in the caryatid's mask-like face, and these combine with Modigliani's lucid sense of form to produce a drawing of great grace and simplicity.

7. Jacques Courtois, known as il Borgognone, *Battle Scene*,
pen and ink, 21.5 × 33 cm (8¹/₂ × 13 in.), GR.214

8. Odilon Redon, *A Throw of the Dice (Un Coup de dès)*, *ca.* 1900,
lithograph, 31 × 24 cm (12¹/₄ × 9¹/₂ in.), GR.193

9. Paul Cézanne

Bathers (Large Plate)
(Baigneurs (Grande Planche)),
ca. 1896–97, lithograph,
43 × 52 cm (17 × 20½ in.), GR.18

Bathers were an ideal subject for an artist preoccupied with depicting nature while paying homage to classical values in art. Cézanne has assembled a scene of four male bathers in various classical poses, set in a shimmering landscape dominated by Mont Sainte-Victoire, the mountain near Aix-en-Provence which he painted obsessively in this later period. The overall composition of the picture is more significant than the execution of its individual elements. The somewhat awkward figures, drawn from memory rather than life, are carefully balanced and integrated into the landscape. The

form of the stretching figure furthest away echoes that of the trees beyond, and the reclining figure's raised knee repeats the rhythm of the mountainous horizon. Cézanne's free and brisk later drawing style transforms the unmoving material world into a pulsating, shifting landscape.

The lithograph is a reworking of the celebrated picture *Bathers at Rest*, which Cézanne had painted twenty-five years earlier, and was commissioned by his agent Ambrose Vollard to promote his work to a wider audience.

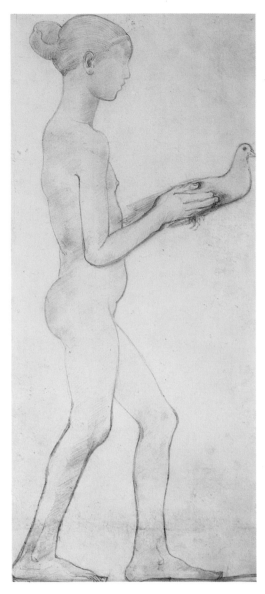

10. Jacob Epstein, *Girl with a Dove, ca.* 1906–07,
pencil, 48 × 21 cm (18⁷/₈ × 8¹/₄ in.), GR.65

11. Pablo Picasso, *Group of Three Women (Groupe de
trois femmes), ca.* 1922–23, drypoint and etching,
17.5 × 12.5 cm (6⁷/₈ × 5 in.), GR.182

12. Edward Burne-Jones, *Study for The Soul Attains, ca.* 1870,
pencil, 30 × 23.8 cm (11³/₄ × 9¹/₄ in.), GR.12

13. Pierre Puvis de Chavannes

Study for The Sacred Grove (Première Pensée du Bois sacré), ca. 1882–83, charcoal on paper on canvas, 57 × 117.5 cm (22½ × 46¼ in.), GR.192

This is a preparatory study for a commission to paint a series of four canvases to decorate the new staircase of the Palais des Arts in Lyons. Puvis was given complete artistic freedom for the project, and drew inspiration from antiquity to create *The Sacred Grove, Beloved of the Arts and Muses of Inspiration,* in which he set three allegorical figures representing the three 'plastic' arts (Painting, Sculpture and Architecture). Surrounding them in a classical landscape were his nine muses of inspiration who describe his own personal vision of the nature of art. The drawing is inscribed *Première*

pensée du bois sacré ('First thoughts for the sacred grove'), which suggests that it marked a crucial moment in the creative process when a satisfactory balance of figures and setting had been achieved. The tranquil and idealized landscape creates a sense of calm, characteristic of Puvis's style. The formal relationships across the long format remained largely unchanged in the finished canvas, which was over 10 m long. Puvis exhibited it at the Salon in Paris in 1884 to great acclaim, before it was installed in Lyons.

14. Ivory Coast, *Heddle pulley from an upright loom, ca.* 19th–20th century, wood, length 22 cm (8¾ in.), GR.332

15. *New Guinean comb (from Southern Coast or Torres Strait), ca.* 19th–20th century, wood, length 34 cm (13⅜ in.), GR.331

16. Roman, *Fragment of a relief, depicting a satyr, ca.* 1st century BC–3rd century AD, terracotta, length 16 cm (6⅜ in.), GR.298

17. New Zealand (Maori people)

Hei-Tiki, Greenstone with mother-of-pearl inlaid eyes, height 12.5 cm (5 in.), GR.324

The Maori name 'Hei-Tiki' means a hanging figure, and the hole at the top of this Hei-Tiki would allow it to be threaded and hung around the neck. They were worn by both men and women and passed down from one generation to the next, acquiring great mana (prestige) and spiritual value. They were sometimes hidden from the eyes of others, or given to the chief of another tribe as a peace offering, to cement a marriage or as a show of supreme hospitality. It could also be a talisman against witchcraft or accident, but their main purpose seems to be as a reminder of departed friends. A Hei-Tiki would be taken off and laid down in the presence of a few friends and wept and sung over, as a way of remembering its owner and the ancestors to whom it has become a memorial. Similarly, the Hei-Tiki would become the focus of rituals marking the return of a long-absent friend, when it would be laid on a clean leaf at the centre of a group, caressed affectionately and called by the name of the returning friend.

The precise significance of the physical form of the Hei-Tiki is debatable. Where indicated, the sex is usually female, and the bowed legs and foetal shape may indicate that it represents fertility or immortality. This Hei-Tiki belonged to Jacob Epstein and was one of thirty fine examples he kept in his unrivalled collection of non-Western art. The Hei-Tiki's smooth design in relief may have influenced his sculpture of the 1913–14 period, when birth and fertility were dominant themes in his work.

18. Jacob Epstein or Charles Holden

Study for the tomb of Oscar Wilde, ca. 1909–11, pencil, 49 × 60 cm (19³/₈ × 23⁵/₈ in.), GR.55

The scandal surrounding the sculptures for the British Medical Association building in the Strand, London (see plate 19), had barely died down before Jacob Epstein found himself in the midst of a fresh outcry over his tomb for Oscar Wilde, for which this is a sketch. Earlier sketches had used curvilinear lines for the winged figure, but the geometric scheme of long phallic-shaped feathers on the final sculpture are clearly shown here. The sketch may have been drawn by the architect Charles Holden, whom Epstein commissioned to design a suitable plinth for the monumental sculpture. Epstein was inspired by the Egyptian art and Assyrian carvings of winged bulls he had seen in the British Museum, and created a sphinx-like angel with arms and legs pushed back by the speed of flight. A dramatic tension was achieved between the sheer physical bulk of the rectangular block of stone and the lightness of the angel in high relief which seems to swoop from it (see fig. 18, p. 28).

When it was finally unveiled in Père Lachaise Cemetery in Paris in 1912 a storm broke out over the angel's well-formed and very male genitalia. It is difficult to imagine Epstein's fury and frustration when his work was first insulted, by the forced addition of a bronze fig leaf, and later censored altogether by being covered entirely by a tarpaulin. Only after the fuss had died down, during the First World War, was the tombstone eventually uncovered.

19. Jacob Epstein

Study for Maternity (for the British Medical Association Building, Strand, London), 1907, pen and ink and pencil, 50 × 30.5 cm (19³/₄ × 12 in.), GR.75

The commission to carve a series of architectural sculptures for Charles Holden's British Medical Association (BMA) building in the Strand, London, was a great opportunity for the young Jacob Epstein. In this preliminary sketch the naturalistic treatment of the subject can be seen in the use of ink to emphasize a flowing line from the head down to the shoulder and back. The final sculpture remained remarkably close to this sketch, but with the significant addition of an infant in the mother's protective arms, increasing the sense of intimacy. With her heavily pregnant profile and modest, inward-tilting head, Epstein realized his vision of heroic woman-hood, and yet, of all the nudes, it was *Maternity* that ignited an explosion of scandal in the press. Anticipating a moral crusade, they declared it outrageous to depict the nudity of a pregnant woman in a public setting.

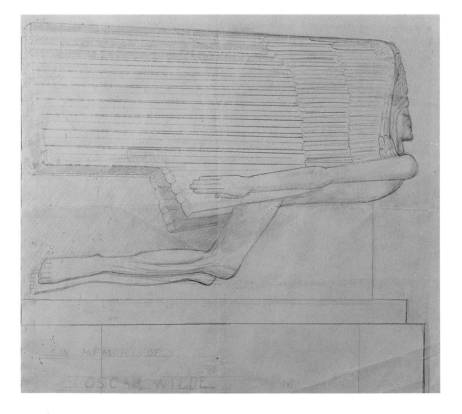

20. Paul Gauguin

Women at the River (Auti Te Pape),
ca. 1891–93, woodcut,
20.3 × 35.3 cm (8 × 13⅞ in.), GR.124

Gauguin carved the wooden block, used to make this print, during his first stay in Tahiti between 1891 and 1893. Tahiti appeared to offer a vision of a simple life and harmony between man and nature which seemed to him unattainable in his native France. He created scenes in which the everyday blends almost imperceptibly with the spiritual. The woman in the foreground is fully described, while the ghostly figure of a woman in the background seems a more spiritual presence.

Gauguin's print, like his painting, breaks with the classical tradition of the time by introducing bold, contrasting patterns and textures within a simple overall design. Finely etched lines, highlighting the figures, contrast with the bolder pattern of deep cuts made to suggest a flowing landscape textured by water and sand. Gauguin's woodcuts heralded a renewed enthusiasm for the medium among the avantgarde artists of the early years of the century, most notably the German Expressionists.

21. Cameroonian (Bamileke Kingdom)

Royal stool, ca. 1920s–30s, wood, height 49 cm (19⅜ in.), diameter 42 cm (16⅝ in.), GR.321

This stool acted as a symbol of Royal Office for a Fon (king) of the Bamileke tribe of the Grassland area of Cameroon. The mere act of sitting on the stool during social occasions was a show of confidence and authority, and linked the Fon with his royal ancestors. It is carved from a single section of timber and supported by a leopard with a broad, snarling mouth. Leopards were symbols of power and leadership, and were closely associated with kingship to the extent that, in mythology, it was said that a king could transform himself into a leopard at will. The leopard is flanked by two royal attendants, one of whom appears to hold a drinking-horn.

Of all the sacred carvings, the stools held the most prestige and could be used by a king to influence all spiritual forces for the benefit of the community. The sculptor who carved the stool was highly regarded, and would have expended much time and energy making it. A tree was carefully selected, felled and seasoned before the design could be roughed out, and was carved and finished several months later. Cameroonian art is prized for its freedom and bold style, and royal stools represent the high point of invention and technical mastery.

22. Jacob Epstein

Study for Rock Drill, ca. 1913,
charcoal, 67.5 × 42.5 cm
(26⅝ × 16¾ in.), GR.72

With its tripod feet and angular body, it is difficult to tell where machine ends and man begins in this early study for the *Rock Drill* sculpture. Epstein's friendships with Modigliani and the Vorticist artist and writer Wyndam Lewis led to a dramatic change in his drawing style, which had previously been characterized by the flowing naturalism of the figures for the British Medical Association building in the Strand, London. His new approach combined his interests in 'primitive', geometric and dynamic elements along with his self-confessed "ardour for machinery". At the time the drawing was made, Epstein saw the *Rock Drill* as an optimistic symbol of power and strength, an image of man and machinery working together with robotic efficiency. The drill has metamorphosed into a symbol of phallic power inspired by African carving, and the lines of force zigzagging beside the figure are like bolts of lightening smashing into the earth.

The *Rock Drill* was eventually realised as a ten-foot-high sculpture in 1915 (see fig. 20, p. 30), with the robotic figure perched high on a real rock drill. Epstein's enthusiasm for the machine age was soon crushed by the mechanical slaughter of the First World War, and his own experience of war led to a nervous breakdown. He discarded the drill and cast only the torso of the figure in bronze, which, with its amputated hands and castrated body, possesses none of the power or optimism of this earlier sketch.

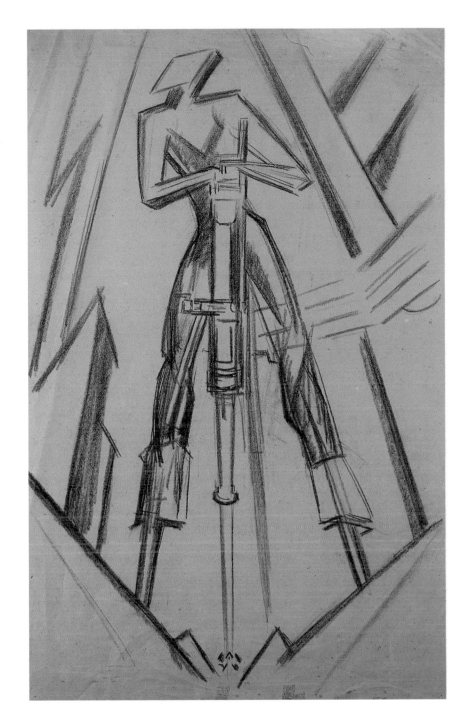

23. Jacob Epstein, *The King of a Rainy Country (Le Roi d'un pays pluvieux)*, illustration for Baudelaire's *Les Fleurs du Mal*, ca. 1933–39, pencil, 56.5 × 43.5 cm (22¼ × 17⅛ in.), GR.58

24. Théodore Géricault, *Study of a Nude Man (Etude d'un homme nu)*, ca. 1816–18, oil on paper on canvas, 30 × 23 cm (11¾ × 9⅛ in.), GR.125

25. Vincent van Gogh

Sorrow, 1882, pencil and pen and ink, 44.5 × 27 cm (17½ × 10⅝ in.), GR.128
ILLUSTRATED OPPOSITE

"How can there be on earth a woman alone, abandoned?" This inscription by Van Gogh, in French below the drawing, a quotation from the contemporary social historian M.J. Michelet, provides a key to this poignant early work. The model was Clasina Maria Hoornik, known as Sien. Van Gogh met her in 1881, when she was pregnant and earning a living as a prostitute. He took her and her child into his home in The Hague, gaining a model in the process. Unlike many of his contemporaries, Van Gogh believed that the cause of prostitution was poverty, a belief shared by some writers such as Michelet. Van Gogh lived out a favourite Victorian fantasy with Sien – charity, forgiveness and rescue – believing that this was all that was needed to change her 'moral character'. Although the image is bleak, the presence of spring flowers in the foreground hint at the possibility of redemption.

The Walsall drawing was highly regarded by the artist, who sent it to his brother Theo saying, "Enclosed is what in my opinion is the best figure I have yet drawn". It was one of three drawings made at the same time, the first drawn from the model, the second and third drawn using the embossed images left on the paper underneath. Only this drawing and one other survive, although he later used the image for a lithograph with the idealistic intention of producing cheap prints as a popular outlet for his work.

Landscapes
and Townscapes

26. Charles Meryon, *The Little Bridge (Le Petit Pont)*, 1850,
etching, 25.5 × 18.75 cm (10¹⁄₈ × 7³⁄₈ in.), GR.166

27. Theodore Garman, *The Thames from Chelsea Embankment*, 1946, pastel,
55.5 × 65.5 cm (21⁷⁄₈ × 25⁷⁄₈ in.), GR.110

28. Theodore Garman, *Summer Garden, South Harting*, 1947,
oil on board, 66 × 76 cm (26 × 30 in.), GR.108

29. Jacob Epstein, *Autumn
Landscape, Epping Forest*, 1933,
watercolour and gouache,
43 cm × 55 cm (17 × 21⅝ in.), GR.68

30. Camille Corot, *The Outskirts of Rome (Les Environs de Rome), ca.* 1865–66, etching, 29 × 21 cm (11½ × 8¼ in.), GR.26

31. Henri-Joseph Harpignies, *Study of Trees*, 1905, black chalk, 21.5 × 27 cm (8½ × 10⅝ in.), GR.137

32. Stanislas Lépine, *The Canal (Le Canal)*, oil on canvas, 21.5 × 30.5 cm (8½ × 12 in.), GR.150

33. Claude Monet

The Sunken Road in the Cliff at Varengeville (Le Chemin creux dans la falaise à Varengeville), 1882
oil on canvas, 60.5 × 73.5 cm
(23⅞ × 29 in.), GR.171

In 1882 Monet moved with his family to Pourville, a small fishing village near Varengeville in Normandy. It marked a period of renewed productivity in his work, inspired by the Normandy coastline. Monet painted several views of this area from both from the top and bottom of the sheer, chalk cliffs, taking the first steps towards what would become the famous 'series' paintings. His view of *The Church at Varengeville*, painted in the same year, can be seen at the Barber Institute of Fine Arts at the University of Birmingham.

Monet was interested in the triangular shapes formed by the meeting of cliffs, sky and sea, and he creates a typically asymmetrical composition here. The building on the left is a coastguard's cottage or customs post which features in other paintings of this period, overlooking the Gorge du Petit Ailly. The pale sky and murky palette reveal Monet's interest in changing light at different times of day and during poor weather conditions.

34. Michael Wishart, *Moths on a Blue Path*, 1963, oil on canvas, 50 × 75 cm (19³/₄ × 29¹/₂ in.), GR.260

35. Pierre-Auguste Renoir, *The Olive Trees at Cagnes-sur-Mers (Les Oliviers à Cagnes-sur-Mer)*, *ca.* 1903–19, oil on canvas, 13 × 11 cm (5¹/₈ × 4³/₈ in.), GR.199

36. Theodore Garman

Stubbers Green Pool, Shelfield,
ca. 1939, pastel, 27 × 35.5 cm
(10⅝ × 14 in.), GR.121

This view of Stubbers Green Pool, in Shelfield, near Walsall, was drawn by Theodore Garman, the son of Jacob Epstein and Kathleen Garman. Rosie Price, the adopted daughter of Kathleen's former nurse, Ada Newbould, and Theodore's constant companion during his visits to Walsall, evokes the scene:

"Theodore's favourite walk was down the lane to Stubbers Green. In those days, beyond the old railway bridge, there were no houses and the road narrowed, hung over with wild flowers and grasses. On hot summer days [Rosie and Theo] enjoyed dawdling along, peeping between the reeds to spy on the ducks, coots and a pair of beautiful swans. There was water on either side right up to the edge of the lane and sometimes it flooded. Occasionally, the great swans crossed their path, lumbering and flapping from one stretch of water to the other. They always built their nest on the smaller stretch of water on the left, a safer place, where the bogs were deep and the reeds high. There was an old boat and Theo rowed Rosie round the little lake. Those were tranquil days, and even when storm clouds gathered Theo never wanted to leave. He taught the child Rosie to look and not be afraid of the black monstrous reflections of clouds in the water."

37. Camille Pissarro, *Landscape, Eragny-sur-Epte*, 1890, watercolour, 12.5 × 17 cm
(5 × 6³/₄ in.), GR.186

38. Walter Sickert, *San Marco, Venice, ca.* 1895–1903, pencil, black chalk and watercolour, 30 × 38 cm
(11³/₄ × 14⁷/₈ in.), GR.236

39. Pierre Bonnard

The River Seine at Vernon (La Seine à Vernon), 1919, oil on canvas, 40.5 × 64 cm (16 × 25¼ in.), GR.7

Bonnard painted this view from the veranda of his house Ma Roulotte, looking down into the Seine Valley. He was fascinated by the river, having explored it by boat and during daily walks, and he painted it many times. Here, he focuses on a view of the river curtained by trees on either side, drawing the eye to the surface of the water as it reflects a cloudy sky. To the right an illusion of depth is created by overlapping trees, painted in progressively darker shades of green, from streaks of vivid colour on the near bank through to the spiky form of an almost black cypress tree beyond. Bonnard's interest in capturing the changing natural light in his river scene reveals the influence of the Impressionists, and the painting does not yet have the appearance of flatness which his later work acquired. However, the acid green and vibrant yellow of the far bank hint at his preference for raising the temperature of the colours he saw in nature.

40. John Constable

Landscape with Clouds, *ca.* 1821–22,
oil on paper on board,
47.5 × 57.5 cm (18¾ × 22⅝ in.),
GR.23

The sky is always a prominent player in Constable's landscapes, and this carefully observed emphatic sky is probably one of a large number he made between 1821 and 1822. The earlier versions tended to include a strip of landscape, but the rich variations of colour through blue and silver-grey to white in this study suggest that the main object was to record the effects of natural light as it filtered through a cloudy sky.

There are several reasons why Constable was particularly sensitive to cloud forms. He was acutely aware of the effect that the sky could have on the mood of a landscape, and he studied the sky in order to use

appropriate lighting and atmosphere in his finished landscapes, without it becoming obtrusive. Constable took a great interest in the scientific ideas of his day, which at this time included the new science of meteorology and the first efforts at classifying and naming types of clouds. His principle was that all paintings should be scientific experiments, and he often noted details of date, time and weather conditions on his cloud sketches. Beyond its significance as the subject of Constable's objective study of nature, the sky also became a focus for his artistic, philosophical and religious ideology and a romantic symbol in its own right.

41. Joseph Mallord William Turner

Carlisle, ca. 1797, pen and ink and watercolour, 11 × 16.5 cm (4³⁄₈ × 6¹⁄₂ in.), GR.245

With its romantic castles, ruins and ancient bridge it is easy to see why Turner was attracted to Carlisle, where he painted this small watercolour. It was probably made during Turner's painting and sketching tour of the North of England in 1797, when he set out to explore the countryside in search of poetic landscapes. Although only twenty-two years old, it is clear that he had already mastered the conventions of the medium, and it was during this period that he began remoulding them to suit his own interests. Scenes such as this were not mere topographical records of places, but were a deliberate framing

of picturesque vistas, carefully selected by the artist. It was a quest for sublime scenery, before which Turner would produce rapid shorthand sketches to be worked up into more finished watercolours, or sold to an engraver, which may account for the slightly restrained style of this work. His interest in the effects of light, picking out the cathedral against a stormy sky, hints at the luminosity and atmosphere of the later romantic landscape painting for which he is famous.

Portraits

42. Henri Matisse, *Woman with an Oriental Veil (Femme avec voilette orientale)*, 1934, pencil, 31 × 23 cm (12¼ × 9⅛ in.), GR.164

43. Jacob Epstein, *Indian Mother and Child, ca.* 1932, pencil, 49 × 56 cm (19⅜ × 22⅛ in.), GR.51

44. Follower of Corneille de Lyon, *Portrait of a Man*, 16th century, oil on panel,
29.5 × 22.5 cm (11⅝ × 8⅞ in.), GR.21

46. Lucian Freud, *Annabel*, 1967, oil on canvas, 35 × 27 cm (13³/₄ × 10⁵/₈ in.), GR.97

45. Jacob Epstein, *Third Portrait of Esther with Flower*, 1949, bronze, height 62 cm (24¹/₂ in.), GR.77

47. Joshua Reynolds

Lieutenant Haswell RN, *ca.* 1746
oil on canvas, 46 × 36 cm
(18⅛ × 14¼ in.), GR.200

The viewer's eye is drawn to the intense gaze of the sitter in this portrait, and over the details of his blue naval uniform. It is just possible to make out a flag and some rope in the background, which also provide clues to his chosen maritime career. Robert Haswell was commissioned as a Lieutenant in the Royal Navy in 1744, when he was a mere fourteen years old, and Reynolds has captured his smooth, youthful complexion. The very young age at which it was possible to purchase a commission as an officer in the navy was a constant source of jokes during this period, from men who resented taking orders from boys. Reynolds was growing in fame as a portrait painter at this time, and, after leaving his native Devon for London, he returned often to paint portraits for the local gentry and naval officers.

LEFT 48. Edouard Manet, *Lola de Valence*, 1862, etching, 23 × 15.75 cm (9¹/₈ × 6¹/₄ in.), GR.162

BELOW LEFT 49. Jacob Epstein, *Kathleen*, 1929, pencil, 54.5 × 44.5 cm (21¹/₂ × 17¹/₂ in.), GR.54

BELOW RIGHT 50. French, *Portrait of a Girl with Curls*, *ca.* 1800–50, black and red chalk, 23 × 20.5 cm (9¹/₈ × 8¹/₈ in.), GR.95

51. Lucian Freud

Portrait of Kitty, 1948–49, oil on board, 35 × 24 cm (13¾ × 9½ in), GR.96

The sitter for this early portrait by Lucian Freud is his first wife, Kitty, whom he married in 1947. Kitty was used to sitting patiently for her portrait, since she was the eldest daughter of Kathleen Garman and Jacob Epstein, and several portraits of her by her father are represented in the Garman Ryan Collection. She possessed the wide-eyed, almost feline features which captivated the artist at the time, and became his frequent model.

The profile format emphasizes Freud's objective approach to portraiture, in which the sitter is scrutinized by both artist and viewer in a cold light against a character-istically bare background. The detail of hair and surface is typical of the meticulous style of his early portraits, and the peeling paint of the shutters reveals his intention to depict the world with all its imperfections, bereft of symbolism or flattery.

52. Peruvian (Mochican people)

Vessel in the form of a man's head,
ca. AD 400–600, clay, height 19.5 cm
(7¾ in.), GR.335

The Mochican people of Peru made this pot in the form of a man's head as a portrait of a person who died, using it in the burial ritual and finally burying it with them. The main body was made by filling a mould with wet clay, which was left to dry until it could be easily removed in two parts, and a stirrup-shaped spout was added which has been broken and lost here. There is also evidence of some incised shaping of the nose and other facial features. The vessel was covered in a clay wash or slip as a ground for the painted decoration made from powdered pigments mixed with water. The headdress and face are coloured with typical red-and-white decoration and a frieze of animals forms a hunting scene across the forehead. The decoration was left to dry and, since glazes were unknown to its maker, it was polished with a hardstone or bone before being fired in an open-pit kiln. Many of these ceramic techniques are still in use in traditional Peruvian pottery today.

ABOVE LEFT 53. Jacob Epstein, *Mask of Rabindranath Tagore*, 1926, bronze, height 50.8 cm (20 in.), GR.82

ABOVE RIGHT 54. Jacob Epstein, *Bust of Meum*, 1918, bronze, height 42 cm (16⅝ in.), GR.79

RIGHT 55. Egyptian, *Mask, believed to be of Queen Nefertiti*, 18th Dynasty, 1350–1300 BC, plaster, height 17 cm (6¾ in.), GR.360

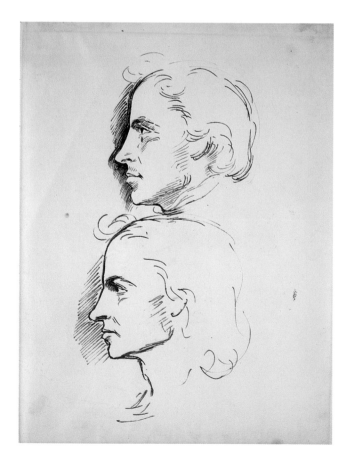

ABOVE LEFT 56. William Makepeace Thackeray, *Self-Portrait*, pencil, 19.5 × 14 cm (7³/₄ × 5⁵/₈ in.), GR.242

ABOVE RIGHT 57. Gianlorenzo Bernini, *Portrait of a Man*, pencil and watercolour, 19.5 × 14.5 cm (7³/₄ × 5³/₄ in.), GR.1

LEFT 58. George Richmond, *Two Portrait Sketches of Samuel Palmer, ca.* 1825–35, pen and ink, 26.5 × 20 cm (10¹/₂ × 7⁷/₈ in.), GR.201

59. Edgar Degas

Portrait of Marguerite, the Artist's Sister (Portrait de Marguerite, soeur de l'artiste), ca. 1856, oil on canvas, 33 × 25 cm (13 × 9⅞ in), GR.33

Degas was the eldest of five children and often enlisted his younger siblings as sitters for his earliest experiments with portraiture. Marguerite is said to have been his favourite, and was about fourteen years old when this portrait was made. Degas admired her fine singing voice, and she bore a striking resemblance to him, with her distinctive nose and slightly asymmetrical eyes. Despite the close bond between them, the subdued palette and dark background lend the image a sombre mood, and pay homage to the severest traditions of European portraiture. Dressed for school, with her hair tightly arranged, Marguerite has an air of stoicism and melancholy. By painting the head large within a small canvas, Degas brings the viewer into close proximity with the sitter. Degas never accepted commissions for portraits and, although he did paint some of the more celebrated figures of his class, those of his family and friends remain his most intimate.

61. Dante Gabriel Rossetti

*Portrait of Elizabeth Siddal, the
Artist's Wife*, ca. 1860, pencil,
23 × 19.5 cm (9⅛ × 7¾ in.), GR.210

Elizabeth Siddal, interrupted while
reading, her impassive face propped
on her hands and her hair
unloosened over her shoulders, gives
away little of her emotional state in
this drawing. Rossetti, a founder-
member of the Pre-Raphaelite
Brotherhood, married Siddal in 1860
after she had been discovered
working in a millinery shop. Her slim
figure, red hair and wide-set, heavy-
lidded eyes caught the attention of
Rossetti's friend, the artist Walter
Deverell. Rossetti produced hundreds
of pencil sketches of Siddal,
informally posed and often reading,
as in this case. He was sympathetic
towards his wife, who suffered from
a nervous disorder and died
prematurely from an overdose of
laudanum in 1862. However,
Rossetti's objective approach to his
sitter tends to ignore her famous wit
and temper, and we learn nothing of
the considerable skill she herself
demonstrated as an artist. This
drawing was hanging in Rossetti's
studio at the time of his death.

69. Anne-Louis Girodet de Roucy Trioson

*Portrait of François-René de
Chateaubriand*, 1791, oil on canvas,
45 × 43.5 cm (17¾ × 17⅛ in.), GR.127

A pupil of the great French
Neoclassical painter David, Girodet
favoured dramatic incident, often
taken from literature, and theatrical
effects of light and shade. One of his
best-known paintings, *The
Entombment of Atala* (1808),
illustrated a scene from a story by
the sitter in this portrait, the French
Romantic writer Chateaubriand.
Lytton Strachey describes the
personality which emerges from
Chateaubriand's work, in the book
Landmarks in French Literature, first
published in 1912: "His conception of
himself was Byronic. He swells forth,
in all his pages, a noble, melancholy,
proud, sentimental creature whom
every man must secretly envy and
every woman passionately adore."
With his shirt rakishly open at the
neck, hair tousled and eyes fixed as
if studying some distant vista,
Chateaubriand is given a suitably
Romantic treatment here.

62. Robert Delaunay

Portrait of Stravinsky (Portrait de Stravinsky), 1918, oil on canvas, 65.5 × 54 cm (25⅞ × 21¼ in.), GR.38

Like the Impressionists before him, Robert Delaunay was interested in the effects of colour and light, and for this portrait of the composer Igor Stravinsky he used washes of paint applied with a free hand, with areas of colour rather than hard lines defining the outline. Delaunay was an important member of the Parisian artistic scene of the pre-1914 period, and was often listed alongside Picasso, Matisse and Derain as one of the leading young French painters of the day. The reason why he is not equally famous today may be because he never truly fitted into any major movement or category.

Delaunay had been trained to paint by a theatre designer, which may explain his later interest in set design. In 1918 he and his wife, Sonia, also a famous artist, were living in Madrid, where they were commissioned by the influential Russian Diaghilev Ballet to create the set and costumes for *Cleopatra*. It was there that they met Stravinsky, who was himself closely involved with the Diaghilev Ballet. They formed a lasting friendship, and this is one of two recorded portraits of Stravinsky by the artist, both painted in the same year. The fact that this portrait remained for many years the possession of the artist's wife is an indication of its value as a reminder of both artist and sitter.

Still Life
and Vessels

63. Eugène Delacroix, *Hollyhock (Rose trémière)*, pencil and watercolour, 15.5 × 9 cm (6⅛ × 3⅝ in.), GR.35

64. Persian, *Turquoise bowl*, Sassanian Dynasty, *ca.* AD 224–651, clay with turquoise glaze, diameter 9 cm (3⅝ in.), GR.315

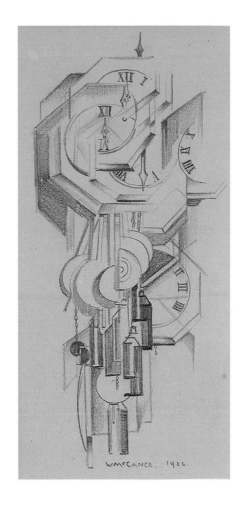

ABOVE LEFT 65. Jan Mankes, *White Orchid*, 1916, oil on board, 24 × 17.5 cm (9½ × 6⅞ in.), GR.356

ABOVE RIGHT 66. William McCance, *Pendulum Clock*, 1926, pencil, 19.5 × 16.5 cm (7¾ × 6½ in.), GR.157

LEFT 67. Egyptian, *Jar with slender ovoid body and ring neck*, Early Dynastic Period *ca.* 2965–2705 BC, alabaster, height 12.5 cm (5 in.), GR.264

68. Jacob Epstein, *Sunflowers*, 1943, watercolour and gouache,
43.5 × 56 cm (17⅛ × 22⅛ in.), GR.69

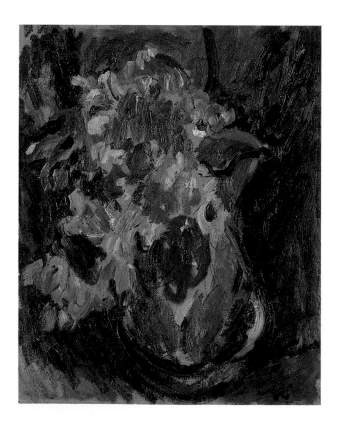

ABOVE 69. Sally Ryan, *Small Flower Painting (Nasturtiums)*,
oil on canvas, 25.5 × 20.5 cm (10⅛ × 8⅛ in.), GR.216

LEFT 70. Matthew Smith, *Flower Piece*, *ca.* 1952–53,
oil on board, 50.5 × 40 cm (19⅞ × 15¾ in.), GR.238

Animals
and Birds

71. Eugène Delacroix, *New Born Lamb*, black chalk, 22 × 17.5 cm
(8 × 6⅞ in.), GR.36

72. Hendrick Goltzius, *A Free and Untamed Horse (Equus Liber et Incopositus)*, 1578,
engraving, 20 × 27 cm (7⅞ × 10⅝ in.), GR.129

73. Jacob Epstein

Sketch of Doves, 1913, black chalk and watercolour, 57 × 44.5 cm (22½ × 17½ in.), GR.64

In 1912, Jacob Epstein settled in the remote village of Pett Level on the Sussex coast, to concentrate on his carving. During this prolific period, he combined the influence of Modigliani and Brancusi with African carving, to express the theme of sexuality with frank acceptance. Doves, as a traditional symbol of love and peace, were a perfect subject for reinterpretation in a style free of sentimentality and focusing instead on the unambiguous act of procreation fundamental to life. Epstein kept birds at his cottage, Bay Point, and this sketch of two doves preening each other appears to be drawn from life. It was then worked up into the more formalized and simplified design of mating doves lower down the page. Epstein invested much effort in his sculptures of doves, carving three pairs in white marble. This sketch closely resembles the second, most successful version.

74. Persian (Luristan), *Finial in the shape of a head of an ibex*, ca. 850–650 BC, bronze, length 11 cm (4⅜ in.), GR.312

75. Chinese, *Incense burner in the shape of a tortoise*, Sung Dynasty, ca. 960–1279, length 19 cm (7½ in.), GR.303

21/75

76. Georges Braque

Birds in Flight, ca. 1953–55, colour lithograph, 24 × 35 cm (9½ × 13¾ in.), GR.9

Birds featured as motifs in Braque's pictures for many years, and became almost an obsession in his later work. Since he refused to attach any symbolic significance to his birds, their meaning has been linked more to Braque's concern with exploring pictorial space. The significance of the sky is emphasized by selecting this as the solid, inked area in the lithograph, rather than the birds, which remain as cut-outs in the air surrounding them. As they beat their wings and soar upwards, from right to left, the birds seem to stir the space through which they move, describing and conveying the properties of the air itself.

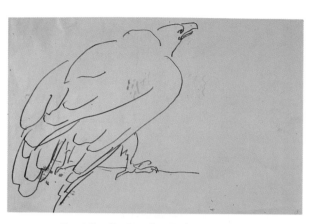

ABOVE 77. Henri Gaudier-Brzeska, *Eagle, ca.* 1912–13, pen and ink, 25 × 35 cm (9⅞ × 13¾ in.), GR.123

RIGHT 78. Georg Ehrlich, *Head of a Deer, ca.* 1957–58, bronze, height 32 cm (12⅝ in.), GR.47

79. Jacob Epstein

Frisky, the Artist's Dog, 1953, bronze, height 31 cm (12¼ in.), GR.86

Jacob Epstein was very fond of his faithful Shetland sheep-dog Frisky, who became his great companion in later life. Frisky's begging pose, with front paws raised, ears back and head lifted, perhaps looking up at her master, describes the dog's temperament. William Garman, Lady Kathleen Epstein's nephew, recalled: "Epstein adored it, he absolutely adored it. Every morning she used to go up to Kensington Gardens, crossing the road at Kensington High Street. Go to the island in the middle of the road, you know where the street lamp is, but look right first and wait there, cross when clear, stop to cross that little bit of island, look left and when clear cross again. She was extraordinary, extraordinary, a lovely dog."

80. Queen Charlotte Islands (Haida people), *Eagle, ca.* 19th–early 20th century, whalebone, height 33 cm (13 in.), GR.322

Children

81. Jacob Epstein, *First Portrait of Esther (with long hair)*, 1944, bronze, height 46 cm (18 1/8 in.), GR.363

82. Jacob Epstein, *The Sisters (Anne and Annabel Freud)*, ca. 1952, bronze, height 18.5 cm (7 3/8 in.), GR.80

83. Sally Ryan, *Nathaniel*, bronze, height 32 cm (12⅝ in.), GR.225

84. Jacob Epstein, *Portrait of Kitty*, 1937, pencil,
56 × 43.5 cm (22¹⁄₈ × 17¹⁄₈ in.), GR.70

85. Jacob Epstein, *Theo*, 1930, pencil, 51 × 39 cm
(20¹⁄₈ × 15³⁄₈ in.), GR.53

86. Edouard Manet, *The Little Girl
(La Petite Fille)*, 1862, etching, 20.5 × 11.5 cm
(8¹⁄₈ × 4¹⁄₄ in.), GR.163

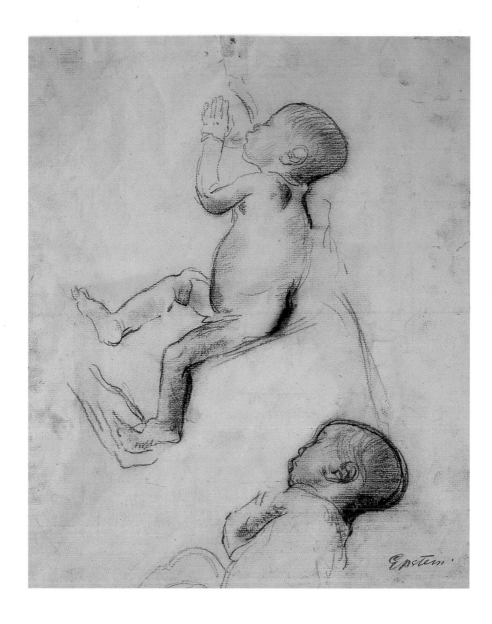

87. Jacob Epstein

Study of a New Born Baby, 1904,
black chalk, 37.5 × 30 cm
(14³/₄ × 11⁷/₈ in), GR.73

This tenderly observed sketch is one of the few works to survive from Epstein's time working and studying in Paris between 1902 and 1905. In 1904 a model carrying her new-born child in her arms came to his studio asking for work. It is perhaps an indication of the furious energy with which he applied himself to his work during this key period that he immediately seized the opportunity provided by their presence. He made several intensely observed studies that succeed in conveying the contrast between the solidity of the child's body and head and the fragility of the limbs. The themes of motherhood and birth were a lifelong preoccupation for Epstein, and although the child's mother is indicated only by faint lines, her presence as the source of nourishment and the force supporting the sleeping form are significant. It was at this point that Epstein's thoughts were turning increasingly towards sculpture, and he was to make bronze sculptures of this baby, both asleep and awake. An example of the latter subject is in the Garman Ryan Collection (see fig. 16, p. 26).

88. Richard Elmore, *Portrait of a Boy*,
oil on canvas, 35 × 28.5 cm
(13¾ × 11¼ in.), GR.50

89. Sally Ryan, *Mother and Child*,
limestone, height 50 cm (19¾ in.), GR.230

90. Camille Pissarro, *Portrait of Félix Pissarro (Portrait de Félix Pissarro)*, 1887, pencil and charcoal, 9.5 × 6 cm (3¾ × 2⅜ in.), GR.185

91. Edwin Landseer, *Young Girl with Pigtails Carrying a Baby*, pencil, 16.5 × 10 cm (6½ × 4 in.), GR.148

92. Alfred Sisley, *The Artist's Son, Pierre*, 1880, pencil, 23 × 31 cm (9⅛ × 12⅞ in.), GR.237

Work
and Leisure

93. Joshua Cristall, *Girl Harvesting Bracken*, ca. 1830, watercolour and gouache, 27 × 19.5 cm (10⅝ × 7¾ in.), GR.30

94. Eugène Boudin, *Figures on the Beach (Personnages sur la plage)*, ca. 1863–65, pencil and watercolour, 14 × 24 cm (5⅝ × 9½ in.), GR.8

95. Albrecht Dürer, *The Men's Bath, ca.* 1497, woodcut, 38.5 × 28 cm (15¼ × 11 in.),
GR.45

ABOVE LEFT 96. Auguste Renoir, *The Country Dance (La Danse à la campagne)*, 1890, etching, 24 × 15 cm (9½ × 5⅞ in.), GR.198

ABOVE RIGHT 97. Horace Mann Livens, *Woman at a Sewing Machine*, black and orange chalk, 30.3 × 20.5 cm (12 × 8⅛ in.), GR.155

LEFT 98. Randolph Caldecott, *Bretton Shepherd with a Sheep*, *ca.* 1879–80, black chalk, 15 × 11 cm (5⅞ × 4⅜ in.), GR.14

99. Samuel Palmer, *The Morning Spread upon the Mountains or The Early Ploughman*, *ca.* 1861, etching, 12.3 × 19.8 cm (4⁷/₈ × 7³/₄ in.), GR.178

100. Raoul Dufy, *Harvest Scene with Steam Threshing Machine*, *ca.* 1943, pencil and watercolour, 28.5 × 45 cm (11¹/₄ × 17³/₄ in.), GR.43

ABOVE LEFT 101. Henri Gaudier-Brzeska, *Women Bearing Sacks*, 1912, plaster, 36 × 28 cm (14¼ × 11 in.), GR.122

ABOVE RIGHT 102. Edouard Vuillard, *The Wet Nurse (La Nourrice)*, black chalk, 23.5 × 16.5cm (9¼ × 6½ in.), GR.248

LEFT 103. Camille Corot, *Woman Reading*, oil on canvas, 30 × 20 cm (11⅞ × 7⅞ in.), GR.27

104. Jean-François Millet, *Going to Work (Allant Travailler)*, 1863, etching, 38.5 × 31 cm (15¼ × 12¼ in.), GR.169

Religion

105. Ben Shahn, *Psalm 133, Dove with Painted Text*, 1960,
watercolour, 26 × 17 cm (10¼ × 6¾ in.), GR.235

106. Robert Bevan, *Breton Women outside a Church, ca.* 1893–94, pencil, pen and ink and
watercolour, 9 × 15 cm (3⅝ × 5⅞ in.), GR.2

107. Italian (Central Italy), *Madonna and Child*, *ca.* 1500, oil and tempera on panel,
44.5 × 34.5 cm (17½ × 13⅝ in.), GR.93

ABOVE LEFT 108. English (Nottingham), *Resurrection*, 15th century, alabaster, 38 × 27 cm (15 × 10⅝ in.), GR.349

ABOVE RIGHT 109. Sir Jacob Epstein, *Maquette for Cavendish Square Madonna and Child*, 1950, lead, halo in bronze, height 35 cm (13¾ in.), GR.91

LEFT 110. Albrecht Dürer, *Christ in Limbo* (from the 'Large Passion' series), 1510, woodcut, 39.5 × 28.5 cm (15⅝ × 11¼ in.), GR.44

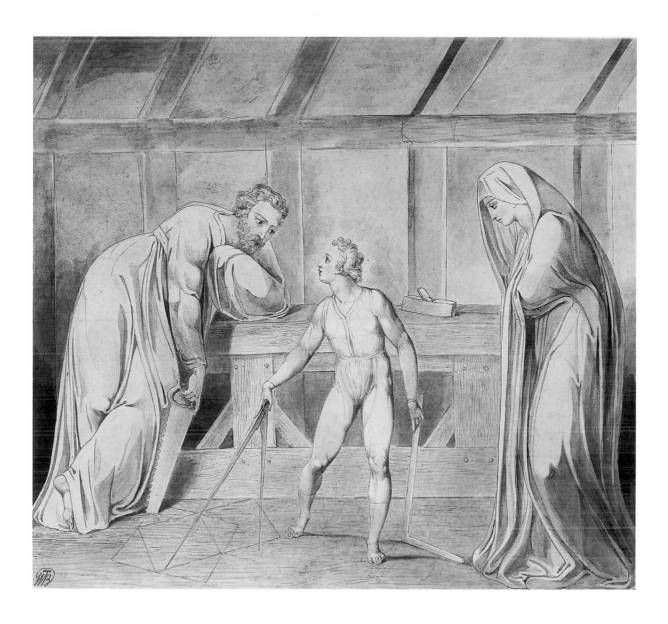

111. William Blake

Christ in the Carpenter's Shop or The Humility of the Saviour, ca. 1803–05, pen and ink and watercolour, 31.5 × 34.5 cm (12³⁄₈ × 13⁵⁄₈ in.), GR.4

The tenderness of this scene comes from the exchange of feeling between the figures. Christ as a youth shows off his knowledge of carpentry by demonstrating a geometric diagram he has drawn on the floor. He seems to search for approval in Joseph's interested and fatherly face, while Mary, balancing the composition, patiently studies her son's drawing. This picture is one of a large number of illustrations of the Bible commissioned for one guinea each by Blake's patron Thomas Butts, eight of which are in the Tate Gallery. The drawing is inscribed with a quotation from St Luke 2:51: "And he went down with them and came to Nazareth and was subject unto them." Blake has interpreted this to mean that, as a member of Mary and Joseph's household, Christ was subject to the environment of a carpenter, who nurtured him and taught him his trade.

For Blake, Christ symbolized imagination and creativity. In this watercolour he is shown mastering the compasses (a symbol of rational knowledge), thereby reconciling the conflicting forces of reason and imagination in humankind.

112. Rembrandt van Rijn, *The Death of the Virgin*, 1639, etching and drypoint, 40.9 × 31.5 cm
(16¹/₈ × 12³/₈ in.), GR.195

113. Lorenzo Salimbeni, known as Lorenzo da San Severino, *An Angel of the Annunciation*, oil on panel, 43 × 17.5 cm (16⁷⁄₈ × 6⁷⁄₈ in.), GR.231

114. French, *Christ with the Crown of Thorns*, *ca.* 12th–14th century, wood, height 36.5 cm (14³⁄₈ in.), GR.346

115 and 116. French (Rouen)

Two pages from a Book of Hours, *ca.* 1480, watercolour and gilt on vellum,
a. 16 × 11 cm (6 × 4³⁄₈ in.),
b. 16.5 × 11 cm (6³⁄₈ × 4³⁄₈ in.),
GR.213a and b
ILLUSTRATED OVERLEAF

In the Middle Ages the term 'Hour' referred to the different portions of the day set aside for religious duties, rather than the precise measurement of time we use today. Books of Hours were produced as personal prayerbooks to allow devout Christians to follow the Church's programme of daily devotion at specific times of the day, and their personal nature is reflected in their small size. They were decorated and gilded with greater or lesser elaboration depending on the owner's wealth, and were symbols of status as well as piety. They were made in workshops by craftsmen and scribes, and no two Books of Hours are the same.

Although not the most ornate of examples, these two pages are from the Hours of the Virgin, the most important and popular images for devotion. The two scenes depicted are *The Angel's Announcement of Christ's Nativity to the Shepherds* (a), and *The Annunciation* (b). The Annunciation is the most significant image of the whole set from a devotional point of view, and was usually finished by the master of the workshop. The creatures inhabiting the borders demonstrate the freedom and inventiveness of the artists, as well as the willingness of their clients to be diverted from their religious texts during long services or periods of private devotion.

117. Georges Rouault, *Three Crosses (Trois Croix)*, 1938, etching, 32.5 × 24 cm (12⅞ × 9½ in.),
GR.211

118. Indian (North Central India)

The Goddess Parvati and attendants,
ca. 11th–12th century, sandstone,
height 27 cm (10⅝ in.), GR.323

This sandstone carving depicts Parvati, one of the most important of the Hindu goddesses and consort of Shiva. As a goddess daughter of the Himalayas she is associated with all mountains, and her name means 'mountain'. Parvati is popularly seen as a mother deity, and she is represented here as benign and peaceful. She is shown in her four-armed form, holding a lotus bud and water-pot in her surviving hands. On either side of her feet are representations of the goddesses Ganga and Yamuna (Jumna), personifications of these two sacred rivers. Her first son, Ganesha, the elephant-headed god of prudence and wisdom, is represented in miniature, next to her upper left hand. This type of medieval sculpture is typical of the kind installed in an outer niche of a temple, as part of a larger and more elaborate sculptural scheme.

Augustus John, *Jacob Epstein, ca.* 1905–06, etching,
13 × 10 cm (5⅛ × 4 in.), GR.142

Garman Ryan Collection: Summary Catalogue

PAINTINGS, PRINTS AND DRAWINGS

Gianlorenzo Bernini (1598–1680)
Portrait of a Man
Pencil and watercolour
19.5 × 14.5 cm (7³/₄ × 5³/₄ in.)
GR.1
Plate 57

Robert Bevan (1865–1925)
Breton Women outside a Church
ca. 1893–94
Pencil, pen and ink and watercolour
9 × 15 cm (3⁵/₈ × 5⁷/₈ in.)
GR.2
Plate 106

The Two-Horse Plough
ca. 1890–94
Black chalk and watercolour
20 × 27.5 cm (7⁷/₈ × 10⁷/₈ in.)
Stamped with artist's monogram: *RPB* (bottom left)
GR.3

William Blake (1757–1827)
Christ in the Carpenter's Shop or The Humility of the Saviour
ca. 1803–05
Pen and ink and watercolour
31.5 × 34.5 cm (12³/₈ × 13⁵/₈ in.)
Signed: *W.B. inv.* (bottom left)
Inscribed: *Luke ch: 2 v: 51 "And He went down with them and came to Nazareth and was subject unto them"*
GR.4
Plate 111

Title Page for The Book of Job
1825
Engraving
21.0 × 16.5 cm (8¹/₄ × 6¹/₂ in.)
Inscribed in the plate: *Invented and Engraved by William Blake, 1825 and London. Published as the Act directs, March 8: 1825 by William Blake, No.3 Fountain Court Strand*
GR.5

Ferdinand Bol (1616–1680)
Hagar at the Well
Pen and ink
17 × 24.5 cm (6³/₄ × 9⁵/₈ in.)
Signed: *rinbran* (bottom left)
GR.196

Richard Parkes Bonington (1802–1828)
Child Study – Miss Montague Cook
Pencil
12 × 12 cm (4³/₄ × 4³/₄ in.)
Signed: *R.P.B* (bottom left)
GR.6

Pierre Bonnard (1867–1947)
The River Seine at Vernon (La Seine à Vernon)
1919
Oil on canvas
40.5 × 64 cm (16 × 25¹/₄ in.)
Signed: *Bonnard* (bottom left)
GR.7
Plate 39

Poster for La Revue Blanche
1894
Lithograph poster
76 × 58.5 cm (29⁷/₈ × 23¹/₈ in.)
Signed and dated on the stone: *Bonnard 94* (centre left)
Inscribed on the stone: *Imp. Edw. Ancourt Paris* (bottom right)
GR.355
Plate 3

Il Borgognone (see Jacques Courtois)

Eugène Boudin (1824–1898)
Figures on the Beach (Personnages sur la plage)
ca. 1863–65
Pencil and watercolour
14 × 24 cm (5⁵/₈ × 9¹/₂ in.)
Stamped: *E.B.* (bottom right)
GR.8
Plate 94

Georges Braque (1882–1963)
Birds in Flight
ca. 1953–55
Lithograph
24 × 35 cm (9¹/₂ × 13³/₄ in.)
Signed: *G. Braque* (bottom margin)
Inscribed: *21/75* (bottom right)
GR.9
Plate 76

René Brô (1930–)
Landscape near Courgeron, Normandy
1962
Oil on canvas
50.5 × 65.5 cm (19⁷/₈ × 25⁷/₈ in.)
Signed and dated: *Brô 62* (centre right)
GR.10

Bernard Buffet (1926–)
Small Girl Reading a Book
Oil on canvas
31 × 26 cm (12¹/₄ × 10¹/₈ in.)
Signed: *Buffet* (reverse)
GR.11

Edward Burne-Jones (1833–1898)
Study for The Soul Attains
ca. 1870
Pencil
30 × 23.8 cm (11³/₄ × 9¹/₄ in.)
GR.12
Plate 12

The Nativity
1887
Pastel
37 × 60 cm (14³/₄ × 23⁵/₈ in.)
Inscribed: *Done at Rottingdean in April 1887 by Sir Ed. Burne-Jones as a design for decoration of a Church at Torquay*
GR.13

**Randolph Caldecott
(1846–1886)**
Breton Shepherd with a Sheep
ca. 1879–80
Black chalk
15 × 11 cm (5⅞ × 4⅜ in.)
GR.14
Plate 98

The Laundry Maid
Watercolour and gouache
19.5 × 12 cm (7¾ × 4¾ in.)
GR.15

Jacques Callot (1592–1635)
Beggar (from the series
Mendiants de Paris)
Pen and ink and wash
14 × 9 cm (5⅝ × 3⅝ in.)
GR.16

Ewan Cameron (1940–)
Still-Life Study
1969
Black chalk and watercolour
25.5 × 34.5 cm
(10⅛ × 13 ⅝ in.)
Inscribed: *Ewan Cameron 1969
Ness House, Fortrose, Rosshire
'Still Life Study'* (reverse)
GR.17

Margaret Cardew (1899–1961)
Normandy Village
Oil on board
28 × 19.5 cm (11 × 7¾ in.)
GR.359

Paul Cézanne (1839–1906)
*Bathers (Large Plate)
(Baigneurs (Grande planche))*
ca. 1896–97
Lithograph
43 × 52 cm (17 × 20½ in.)
Signed on the stone:
P. Cézanne (bottom right)
GR.18
Plate 9

**Alexander Chisholm
(ca. 1792/3–1847)**
*Sir Walter Scott with his Dog,
Bran*
Black chalk
19 × 15 cm (7½ × 5⅞ in.)
GR.20

**In the style of Jean Clouet
(ca. 1485–1541/2)**
Portrait of a Lady
Pencil, watercolour and chalk
32 × 21 cm (12⅝ × 8¼ in.)
GR.22

John Constable (1776–1837)
Landscape with Clouds
ca. 1821–22
Oil on paper on board
47.5 × 57.5 cm (18¾ × 22⅝in.)
GR.23
Plate 40

Ash Tree
Pencil
25 × 16.5 cm (9⅞ × 6 in.)
GR.24

**Follower of Corneille de Lyon
(ca. 1500/10–1575)**
Portrait of a Man
Oil on panel
29.5 × 22.5 cm (11⅝ × 8⅞ in.)
GR.21
Plate 44

**Jean-Baptiste Camille Corot
(1796–1875)**
Study of a Beech Tree
Pencil
22 × 20 cm (8¾ × 7⅞ in.)
Inscribed: *COROT* (bottom left)
GR.25

*The Outskirts of Rome
(Les Environs de Rome)*
ca. 1865–66
Etching
29 × 21 cm (11½ × 8¼ in.)
GR.26
Plate 30

Woman Reading
Oil on canvas
30 × 20 cm (11⅞ × 7⅞ in.)
GR.27
Plate 103

**Jacques Courtois, known as
il Borgognone (1621–1675)**
Battle Scene
Pen and ink
21.5 × 33 cm (8½ × 13 in.)
GR.214
Plate 7

Joseph Crawhall (1861–1913)
Stork
Pencil
20.5 × 15 cm (8⅛ × 5⅞ in.)
GR.28

**Joshua Cristall
(ca. 1767/9–1847)**
*Pastoral Family with a White
Cow*
Watercolour
22.5 × 34 cm (8⅞ × 13⅜ in.)
GR.29

Girl Harvesting Bracken
ca. 1830
Watercolour and gouache
27 × 19.5 cm (10⅝ × 7¾ in.)
Inscribed with artist's
monogram (bottom left)
GR.30
Plate 93

**Henri-Edmond Cross
(1856–1910)**
Dancing Female Figures
1890
Pencil, crayon and pastel
22 × 40.5 cm (8¾ × 16 in.)
Stamped: *H.E.C.* (bottom left)
Inscribed: *H.E. Cross 1890*
(reverse)
GR.31

Edgar Degas (1834–1917)
*Portrait of Marguerite, the
Artist's Sister (Portrait de
Marguerite, soeur de l'artiste)*
ca. 1856
Oil on canvas
33 × 25 cm (13 × 9⅞ in.)
GR.33
Plate 59

Eugène Delacroix (1798–1863)
Hollyhock (Rose trémière)
Pencil and watercolour
15.5 × 9 cm (6⅛ × 3⅝ in.)
GR.35
Plate 63

New Born Lamb
Black chalk
22 × 17.5 cm (8¾ × 6⅞ in.)
Stamped: E.D (bottom right)
GR.36
Plate 71

A Blacksmith (Un Forgeron)
1833
Etching and aquatint
24 × 18 cm (9½ × 7⅛ in.)
Stamped on the plate with
artist's monogram: *ED* (top
right)
GR.37

Robert Delaunay (1885–1941)
*Portrait of Stravinsky
(Portrait de Stravinsky)*
1918
Oil on canvas
65.5 × 54 cm (25⅞ × 21¼ in.)
GR.38
Plate 62

**Narcisse Virgile Diaz de la
Peña (1807–1876)**
The Wood Gatherer
Oil on canvas
45 × 22 cm (17¾ × 8¾ in.)
Signed: *N. Diaz* (bottom left)
GR.39

**Jan van Diest
(early 16th century)**
Trees in Summer
Pencil
16.5 × 12.5 cm (6½ × 5 in.)
GR.40

Francis Dodd (1874–1949)
Clouds, Hills and Fields
1902
Watercolour and gouache
19 × 28.5 cm (7½ × 11¼ in.)
Signed and dated: *F. Dodd
1902* (bottom right)
GR.41

Domenichino (see Zampieri)

Raoul Dufy (1877–1953)
*Harvest Scene with Steam
Threshing Machine*
ca. 1943
Pencil and watercolour
28.5 × 45 cm (11¼ × 17¾ in.)
Signed: *Raoul Dufy* (bottom
left)
GR.43
Plate 100

Albrecht Dürer (1471–1528)
Christ in Limbo (from the
'Large Passion' series)
1510
Woodcut
39.5 × 28.5 cm (15⅝ × 11¼ in.)
Signed and dated in the block:
AD (bottom centre) *1510*
(centre right)
GR.44
Plate 110

The Men's Bath
ca. 1497
Woodcut
38.5 × 28 cm (15¼ × 11 in.)
Signed in the block: *AD*
(bottom centre)
GR.45
Plate 95

The Last Supper (from the
'Large Passion' series)
1510
Woodcut
40 × 29 cm (15¾ × 11½ in.)
Signed and dated in the block:
AD 1510 (bottom centre)
GR.46

William Ellis (fl. 1858–1895)
*A Lane at Hamstead,
Staffordshire*
Oil on canvas
51 × 61 cm (20⅛ × 24 in.)
GR.49

Richard Elmore (fl. 1852–1885)
Portrait of a Boy
Oil on canvas
35 × 28.5 cm (13¾ × 11¼ in.)
GR.50
Plate 88

Jacob Epstein (1880–1959)
Indian Mother and Child
ca. 1932
Pencil
49 × 56 cm (19⅜ × 22⅛ in.)
Signed: *Epstein* (bottom left)
GR.51
Plate 43

The Blessing
1930
Pencil and watercolour
43 × 56 cm (17 × 22⅛ in.)
Signed and dated: *Epstein
1930* (bottom right)
GR.52

Theo
1930
Pencil
51 × 39 cm (20⅛ × 15⅜ in.)
Signed: *Epstein* (bottom right)
GR.53
Plate 85

Kathleen
1929
Pencil
54.5 × 44.5 cm (21½ × 17½ in.)
Signed: *Epstein* (bottom right)
GR.54
Plate 49

*Figure Study, Male Nude
(Adam)*
1934
Pencil and watercolour
41.5 × 55.5 cm (16⅜ × 21⅞ in.)
Signed: *Epstein* (bottom right)
GR.56

Two Heads (Pietà)
1932
Pencil
42 × 56 cm (16⅝ × 22⅛ in.)
Signed: *Epstein* (bottom right)
GR.57

*The King of a Rainy Country
(Le Roi d'un pays pluvieux) –
Illustration for Baudelaire's
Les Fleurs du Mal*
ca. 1933–39
Pencil
56.5 × 43.5 cm (22¼ × 17⅛ in.)
Signed: *Epstein* (bottom right)
GR.58
Plate 23

*The Risen Christ or "Noli me
tangere"*
1930
Pencil
56.5 × 43 cm (22¼ × 17 in.)
GR.59

Reclining Model (Sunita, Nude)
Pencil
36.5 × 46 cm (14⅜ × 18⅛ in.)
Signed: *Epstein* (top centre)
GR.60

Sunita
ca. 1930
Charcoal on cardboard
61 × 44 cm (24 × 17⅜ in.)
GR.61

Head of Nan
1909
Pencil
48 × 33.5 cm (18⅞ × 13½ in.)
GR.62

Self-Portrait
ca. 1901
Red chalk
29.5 × 22.5 cm (11⅝ × 8⅞ in.)
GR.63

Sketch of Doves
1913
Black chalk and watercolour
57 × 44.5 cm (22½ × 17½ in.)
GR.64
Plate 73

Girl with a Dove
ca. 1906–07
Pencil
48 × 21 cm (18⅞ × 8¼ in.)
GR.65
Plate 10

Profile of a Young Girl
1906
Pencil
46.5 × 29.5 cm (18⅜ × 11⅝ in.)
GR.66

Children Resting
1901
Red chalk
21.5 × 29 cm (8½ × 11½ in.)
GR.67

*Autumn Landscape, Epping
Forest*
1933
Watercolour and gouache
43 × 55 cm (17 × 21⅝ in.)
Signed: *Epstein* (bottom left)
GR.68
Plate 29

Sunflowers
1943
Watercolour and gouache
43.5 × 56 cm (17⅛ × 22⅛ in.)
Signed: *Epstein* (bottom left)
GR.69
Plate 68

Portrait of Kitty
1937
Pencil
56 × 43.5 cm (22⅛ × 17⅛ in.)
Signed: *Epstein* (bottom right)
GR.70
Plate 84

Nan Seated (Nude)
1911
Pencil
54 × 46.5 cm (21¼ × 18⅜ in.)
Signed: *Epstein* (bottom right)
GR.71

Study for Rock Drill
ca. 1913
Charcoal
67.5 × 42.5 cm (26⅝ × 16¾ in.)
GR.72
Plate 22

Study of a New Born Baby
1904
Black chalk
37.5 × 30 cm (14¾ × 11⅞ in.)
Signed: *Epstein* (bottom right)
GR.73
Plate 87

Men with Mice and Birds
ca. 1901
Black chalk
59.5 × 41 cm (23½ × 16⅛ in.)
Signed: *Epstein* (bottom right)
GR.74

Study for Maternity (for the
British Medical Association
Building, Strand, London)
1907
Pen and ink and pencil
50 × 30.5 cm (19¾ × 12 in.)
Inscribed: *Parvati* (top right)
GR.75
Plate 19

*The Sweat Shop or Lunch in
the Shop*
ca. 1901–02
Black chalk
53 × 43 cm (20⅞ × 17 in.)
Signed: *Jacob Epstein* (bottom
left)
GR.76

Jacob Epstein (1880–1959) or Charles Holden (1875–1960)
Study for the tomb of Oscar Wilde
ca. 1909–11
Pencil
49 × 60 cm (19³⁄₈ × 23⁵⁄₈ in.)
Inscribed: *IN MEMORY OF OSCAR WILDE* (bottom left)
GR.55
Plate 18

William Etty (1787–1849)
Standing Female Nude
ca. 1835–40
Oil on canvas
69 × 52.5 cm (27¹⁄₄ × 20³⁄₄ in.)
GR.92

Newton Fielding (1797–1856)
Russet Trees with a Pool
Watercolour
18.5 × 28.5 cm (7³⁄₈ × 11¹⁄₄ in.)
GR.152

In the style of Myles Birket Foster (1825–1899)
Children Playing in a Wood
ca. 1867
Watercolour and gouache
14.5 × 25 cm (5³⁄₄ × 9⁷⁄₈ in.)
Signed with the artist's monogram and dated: *1867* (bottom left)
GR.94

French
Portrait of a Girl with Curls
ca. 1800–50
Black and red chalk
23 × 20.5 cm (9¹⁄₈ × 8¹⁄₈ in.)
GR.95
Plate 50

French (Rouen)
Two pages from a Book of Hours
ca. 1480
Watercolour and gilt on vellum
a. 16 × 11 cm (6 × 4³⁄₈ in.)
b. 16.5 × 11 cm (6³⁄₈ × 4³⁄₈ in.)
GR.213a and b
Plates 115 and 116

Lucian Freud (1922–)
Portrait of Kitty
1948–49
Oil on board
35 × 24 cm (13³⁄₄ × 9¹⁄₂ in.)
Signed and dated: *Lucian Freud 1948–1949* (top right)
GR.96
Plate 51

Annabel
1967
Oil on canvas
35 × 27 cm (13³⁄₄ × 10⁵⁄₈ in.)
GR.97
Plate 46

Kingcups – Souvenir of Glen Artney
1967
Oil on canvas
24 × 19 cm (9¹⁄₂ × 7¹⁄₂ in.)
GR.98

Sleeping Girl
1961
Watercolour
33 × 23.5 cm (13 × 9¹⁄₄ in.)
GR.99

Othon Friesz (1879–1949)
Still Life with Fruit
Pen and ink and watercolour
19 × 25 cm (7¹⁄₂ × 9⁷⁄₈ in.)
GR.100

Eugène Fromentin (1820–1876)
Head of an Old Woman
Oil on board
17 × 13 cm (6³⁄₄ × 5¹⁄₈ in.)
GR.101

Arab Horses
Pencil
14 × 23.5 cm (5⁵⁄₈ × 9¹⁄₄ in.)
Stamped: *Vente Fromentin* (bottom left)
GR.102

George Frost (1754–1821)
Trees in a Hedgerow
Pencil
15.5 × 17.5 cm (6¹⁄₈ × 6⁷⁄₈ in.)
GR.104

Circle of Thomas Gainsborough (1727–1788)
Beech Trees
Black and white chalk
39.5 × 27.5 cm (15⁵⁄₈ × 10⁷⁄₈ in.)
GR.103

Clive Gardiner (1891–1960)
The Hamlet, Scilly Isles
1955
Oil on board
13 × 14.5 cm (5¹⁄₈ × 5³⁄₄ in.)
GR.105

The Blue Boat
Pen and ink and coloured chalk
19.5 × 22 cm (7⁵⁄₈ × 8⁵⁄₈ in.)
GR.106

Theodore Garman (1924–1954)
Window Picture in June
Oil on canvas
183 × 122 cm (72¹⁄₈ × 48¹⁄₈ in.)
GR.107

Summer Garden, South Harting
1947
Oil on board
66 × 76 cm (26 × 30 in.)
Signed: *Theo Garman* (bottom left)
GR.108
Plate 28

Arum Lilies (Easter Flowers)
1949
Oil on canvas
99 × 128 cm (39³⁄₈ × 50³⁄₈ in.)
GR.109

The Thames from Chelsea Embankment
1946
Pastel
55.5 × 65.5 cm (21⁷⁄₈ × 25⁷⁄₈ in.)
Signed: *Theodore Garman* (bottom right)
GR.110
Plate 27

Stefanie
1951
Pencil and chalk
40.5 × 35 cm (16 × 13³⁄₄ in.)
GR.111

Old Graveyard, King's Road, Chelsea
1945
Pastel
47.5 × 60.5 cm (18³⁄₄ × 23⁷⁄₈ in.)
GR.112

Paolo Vivante
Black chalk
50.5 × 37.5 cm (19⁷⁄₈ × 14³⁄₄ in.)
GR.113

Villa Solaia
1949
Oil on canvas
91.5 × 142 cm (36 × 55⁷⁄₈ in.)
GR.114

The Blue Girl
1948
Oil on canvas
121.5 × 91.5 cm (47⁷⁄₈ × 36 in.)
GR.115

Autumn Still Life
Oil on canvas
127 × 102 cm (50 × 40¹⁄₄ in.)
GR.116

Good Friday
1952
Oil on canvas
80 × 64 cm (31¹⁄₂ × 25¹⁄₄ in.)
GR.117

Roland Joffé
ca. 1950
Pastel
62 × 47 cm (24¹⁄₂ × 18¹⁄₂ in.)
Signed: *Theodore Garman* (bottom right)
Inscribed: *Rowland* (bottom right)
GR.118

The Sick Child
ca. 1940
Pastel
38 × 50 cm (15 × 20¹⁄₈ in.)
Signed: *Theodore Garman* (bottom left)
GR.119

Grada van Henglaas
Pastel
76 × 55.5 cm (30 × 21⅞ in.)
Signed: *Theodore Garman*
(bottom left)
Inscribed: *Grada van Henglaas*
(bottom right)
GR.120

Stubbers Green Pool, Shelfield
ca. 1939
Pastel
27 × 35.5 cm (10⅝ × 14 in.)
Signed: *THEODORE GARMAN*
(bottom left)
GR.121
Plate 36

**Henri Gaudier-Brzeska
(1891–1915)**
Eagle
ca. 1912–13
Pen and ink
25 × 35 cm (9⅞ × 13¾ in.)
GR.123
Plate 77

Paul Gauguin (1848–1903)
*Women at the River (Auti Te
Pape)*
ca. 1891–93
Woodcut
20.3 × 35.3 cm (8 × 13⅞ in.)
Signed on the block: *P G O*
(bottom left)
Inscribed on the block: *AUTI
TE PAPE* (bottom right)
GR.124
Plate 20

**Théodore Géricault
(1791–1824)**
*Study of a Nude Man (Etude
d'un homme nu)*
ca. 1816–18
Oil on paper on canvas
30 × 23 cm (11¾ × 9⅛ in.)
GR.125
Plate 24

A French Farrier
ca. 1821
Lithograph
24.25 × 35.5 cm (9⅝ × 14 in.)
Inscribed on the stone:
J. Géricault invt. (bottom left),
*A FRENCH FARRIER and C.
Hullmandel's Lithography*
(bottom right)
GR.126

**Anne-Louis Girodet de Roucy
Trioson (1767–1824)**
*Portrait of François-René de
Chateaubriand*
1791
Oil on canvas
45 × 43.5 cm (17¾ × 17⅛ in.)
Signed: *Girodet* (centre right)
GR.127
Plate 60

Vincent van Gogh (1853–1890)
Sorrow
1882
Pencil, pen and ink
44.5 × 27 cm (17½ × 10⅝ in.)
Signed: *Vincent del.* (bottom
left)
Inscribed: *Sorrow* (bottom
right) and *Comment se fait-il
qu'il y ait sur la terre une
femme seule – Délaissée.
Michelet* (bottom margin)
GR.128
Plate 25

Hendrick Goltzius (1558–1617)
*A Free and Untamed Horse
(Equus Liber et Incopositus)*
1578
Engraving
20 × 27 cm (7⅞ × 10⅝ in.)
Signed on the plate:
H. Goltzius fe. (bottom right)
Inscribed on the plate: *EQUUS
LIBER ET INCOPOSITUS* (top
left), *Jo. Strada inv., P.Galleus
excu.* (bottom left), *Hic
bellator equus Campo sese
arduus infert In precepsqr fuit.
stricte contemptor habene,
Frena pati indocilis: sed
tandem tempore lento, Et
facilis dextra moderatus paret
habenis.* (bottom margin)
GR.129
Plate 72

Francisco de Goya (1746–1828)
*Margarita of Austria, Queen of
Spain (after Velázquez)*
1778
Etching
39.5 × 32.5 cm (15⅝ × 12⅞ in.)
Inscribed on the plate: *D.
Margarita de Austria Reyna de
España, Muger de Phelipe III.
Pintura de D. Diego Velazquez
del tamaño del natural en el
Real Palacio de Madrid,
dibujada y grabada por D.
Fran.co Goya Pintor, año de
1778* (bottom margin)
GR.130

*Grotesque Dance (Baile
grotesco)*, from the
'Disparates/Proverbios' series
ca. 1819–20
Etching
25 × 36 cm (9⅞ × 14¼ in.)
GR.131
Plate 2

Blockhead (Bubulicón), from
the 'Disparates/Proverbios'
series
ca. 1819–1820
Etching
25 × 35.5 cm (9⅞ × 14 in.)
GR.132

Kate Greenaway (1846–1901)
Child with a Parrot (Illustration
for *Little Folks* magazine)
ca. 1877
Pen and ink and watercolour
8.5 × 8 cm (3⅜ × 3⅛ in.)
GR.133

Child with a Dog (Illustration
for *Little Folks* magazine)
ca. 1877
Pen and ink and watercolour
8.5 × 8 cm (3⅜ × 3⅛ in.)
Signed: *KG* (bottom right)
GR.134

Constantin Guys (1802–1892)
Dandies in the Park
Pen and ink and watercolour
17 × 23 cm (6¾ × 9⅛ in.)
GR.135

William Hamilton (1751–1801)
The Apple Picker
1790
Black and red chalk
16.5 × 15 cm (6½ × 5⅞ in.)
GR.136

**Henri-Joseph Harpignies
(1819–1916)**
Study of Trees
1905
Black chalk
21.5 × 27 cm (8½ × 10⅝ in.)
Signed and dated: *Harpignies
1905* (bottom left)
GR.137
Plate 31

John Hayter (1800–1891)
*Harriet's First Gallop on
Plumstead Heath*
1853
Pen and ink
15.5 × 19.5 cm (6⅛ × 7¾ in.)
Inscribed: *Harriet's First Gallop
on Plumstead Heath*, *Sept 28,
1853, Norfolk* (bottom margin)
GR.138

Charles Hett (1941–)
Landscape in Norfolk
Acrylic on hardboard
38 × 35.5 cm (15 × 14 in.)
GR.139

**Circle of William Hoare
(ca. 1707–1792)**
The Three Graces
Red and black chalk
18.5 × 16.5 cm (7³⁄₁₀ × 6½ in.)
GR.140

Italian (Central Italy)
Madonna and Child
ca. 1500
Oil and tempera on panel
44.5 × 34.5 cm (17½ × 13⅝ in.)
GR.93
Plate 107

Italian (Lombardy)
*Saint Carlo Bartolommeo in
Adoration Before a Crucifix*
17th century
Oil on copper
24.5 × 19.5 cm (9⅝ × 7¾ in.)
Inscribed: *Mattheus Rossellius
Florentis Fecit. M.D. CXVI*
(reverse)
GR.241

Augustus John (1878–1961)
Jacob Epstein
ca. 1905–1906
Etching
13 × 10 cm (5⅛ × 4 in.)
Signed: *John* (bottom right)
GR.142
See page 112

W.B. Yeats
1909
Etching
17.5 × 12.5 cm (6⅞ × 5 in.)
Signed and dated on the
plate: *John 09* (centre right);
also signed: *John* (bottom
right)
GR.143

Female Figure Study
Black chalk
24.5 × 34.5 cm (9⅝ × 13⅝ in.)
Signed: *John* (centre right)
GR.144

**Johan Barthold Jongkind
(1819–1891)**
*Windmills in Holland
(Moulins en Hollande)*
1867
Etching
13.5 × 19 cm (5⅜ × 7½ in.)
Signed and dated on the
plate: *Rotterdam 1867
Jongkind* (bottom right)
GR.145

Celso Lagar (1891–1966)
River Scene with a Bridge
Pencil and watercolour
12 × 20 cm (4¾ × 7⅞ in.)
Stamped: *Lagar* (bottom
centre)
GR.146

Nude (Seated Woman)
Pen and ink and watercolour
30 × 19 cm (11⅞ × 7½ in.)
Stamped: *Lagar* (bottom right)
GR.147

Edwin Landseer (1802–1873)
*Young Girl with Pigtails
Carrying a Baby*
Pencil
16.5 × 10 cm (6½ × 4 in.)
GR.148
Plate 91

Study of Wayside Plants
1866
Oil on paper
26.5 × 33 cm (10½ × 13 in.)
Dated: *Aug. 27. 1866* (centre)
GR.149

Paul Lecuit Monroy (1858–?)
Autumn River Scene, Bougival
1920
Watercolour
18.5 × 29.25 cm (7⅜ × 11⅝ in.)
Signed and dated: *P. Lecuit
Monroy Bougival 9-10-1920*
(bottom right)
GR.172

Stanislas Lépine (1835–1892)
The Canal (Le Canal)
Oil on canvas
21.5 × 30.5 cm (8½ × 12 in.)
Signed: *S. Lépine* (bottom
right)
GR.150
Plate 32

Lucas van Leyden (1494–1533)
Esther Before Ahasuerus
1518
Engraving
27 × 22 cm (10⅝ × 8¾ in.)
Signed and dated on the
plate: *L. 1518* (bottom centre)
GR.151

**Circle of John Linnell
(1792–1882)**
Nude Girl by a Pool
Pencil and watercolour
9.5 × 12.5 cm (3¾ × 5 in.)
Inscribed: *PL. B4. 97* (bottom
right)
GR.153

**Horace Mann Livens
(1862–1936)**
*Mother and Children on a
Windy Heath*
1903
Black chalk, watercolour and
gouache
26.5 × 35.5 cm (10½ × 14 in.)
Signed and dated: *H.M. Livens
03* (bottom left)
GR.154

Woman at a Sewing Machine
Black and orange chalk
30.3 × 20.5 cm (12 × 8⅛ in.)
GR.155
Plate 97

Maximilien Luce (1858–1941)
Market Scene
ca. 1896
Pastel and coloured crayon
37.5 × 25.5 cm (14¾ × 10⅛ in.)
Signed: *Luce* (bottom right)
Inscribed: *a Pelles* (bottom
right)
GR.156

William McCance (1894–1970)
Pendulum Clock
1926
Pencil
19.5 × 16.5 cm (7¾ × 6½ in.)
Signed and dated:
W. McCANCE 1926 (bottom
right)
GR.157
Plate 66

Ambrose McEvoy (1878–1927)
Dieppe Street Scene
Oil on canvas
62.5 × 52 cm (24⅝ × 20½ in.)
GR.158

The Letter
ca. 1905
Oil on canvas
50.5 × 40.5 cm (19⅞ × 16 in.)
GR.159

Windmill with a Farm
Pencil, watercolour and
gouache
24 × 38 cm (9½ × 15 in.)
GR.160

Mary McEvoy, the Artist's Wife
ca. 1910
Charcoal and coloured chalk
45.5 × 28.5 cm (18 × 11¼ in.)
GR.161

Edouard Manet (1832–1883)
Lola de Valence
1862
Etching
23 × 15.75 cm (9⅛ × 6¼ in.)
Signed in the plate: *ed Manet*
(bottom left)
Inscribed on the plate: *Entre
tant de beautés que partout
on peut voir Je comprend bien,
amis, quelle Désir balance
Mais on voit scintiller dans
Lola de Valence Le charme
inattendu d'un bijou rose et
noir (Ch. Baudelaire)* (bottom
margin)
GR.162
Plate 48

The Little Girl (La Petite Fille)
1862
Etching
20.5 × 11.5 cm (8⅛ × 4¼ in.)
Signed in the plate: *ed Manet*
(top left)
GR.163
Plate 86

Jan Mankes (1889–1920)
White Orchid
1916
Oil on board
24 × 17.5 cm (9½ × 6⅞ in.)
GR.356
Plate 65

Henri Matisse (1869–1954)
*Woman with an Oriental Veil
(Femme avec voilette
orientale)*
1934
Pencil
31 × 23 cm (12¼ × 9⅛ in.)
Signed and dated: *Henri
Matisse 34* (bottom right)
GR.164
Plate 42

Charles Meryon (1821–1868)
*Little Tower on the Rue de la
Tixeranderie (Tourelle de la
rue de la Tixeranderie)*
1852
Etching
24.5 × 12.5 cm (9⅜ × 5 in.)
Signed on the plate: *CM*
(top right)
GR.165

The Little Bridge (Le Petit Pont)
1850
Etching
25.5 × 18.75 cm (10⅛ × 7⅜ in.)
Signed on the plate: *CM* (top right)
Inscribed on the plate: *publié par l'artiste* (bottom left) *Le Petit Pont* (bottom centre) *Imp. à Delaitre Rue St Jacque 171* (bottom right)
GR.166
Plate 26

Jean-François Millet (1814–1875)
Woman Carding Wool (La Cardeuse)
ca. 1855
Pencil
25 × 19 cm (9⅞ × 7½ in.)
Stamped with the artist's initials: *J.F.M.* (bottom right)
GR.167

The Charcoal Burner's Hut (Cabane du charbonnier)
Charcoal
27 × 40 cm (10⅝ × 15¾ in.)
Signed: *JFM* (bottom left)
GR.168

Going to Work (Allant Travailler)
1863
Etching
38.5 × 31 cm (15¼ × 12¼ in.)
Signed on the plate: *J.F. Millet* (bottom left)
GR.169
Plate 104

Amedeo Modigliani (1884–1920)
Caryatid (Cariatide)
ca. 1913–14
Pencil and blue crayon
55 × 41.5 cm (21⅝ × 16⅜ in.)
Signed: *Modigliani* (bottom right)
GR.170
Plate 6

Claude Monet (1840–1926)
The Sunken Road in the Cliff at Varengeville (Le Chemin creux dans la falaise à Varengeville)
1882
Oil on canvas
60.5 × 73.5 cm (23⅞ × 29 in.)
Signed: *Claude Monet* (bottom left)
GR.171
Plate 33

George Morland (ca. 1763–1804)
Studies of a Horse
Pencil
15.5 × 21.5 cm (6⅛ × 8½ in.)
Signed: *George Morland* (top left)
GR.173

Fritz Mühsam (ca. 1882–1949)
Esther
1934
Oil on canvas
46 × 38.5 cm (18⅛ × 15¼ in.)
GR.174

Theo
1934
Oil on canvas
41.5 × 33.5 cm (16⅜ × 13¼ in.)
Signed: *Muhsam* (bottom left)
GR.175

Alfred Munnings (1878–1959)
The Rue Géricault, Rouen
1918
Pencil
22 × 18 cm (8¾ × 7⅛ in.)
Signed and dated: *A.J. MUNNINGS Rue Géricault, Rouen, 23:6:18* (bottom right)
GR.176

François Navez (1787–1869)
A Rest in the Fields (Repos aux champs)
ca. 1845
Charcoal
25.5 × 36 cm (10⅛ × 14¼ in.)
GR.177

Samuel Palmer (1805–1881)
The Morning Spread upon the Mountains or The Early Ploughman
ca. 1861
Etching
12.3 × 19.8 cm (4⅞ × 7¾ in.)
Signed: *S. Palmer* (bottom right margin)
GR.178
Plate 99

Opening the Fold or Early Morning
1880
Etching
11.75 × 15.5 cm (4 ⅝ × 6⅛ in.)
Signed on the plate: *S. PALMER INVNT* (bottom left)
GR.179

Jules Pascin (1885–1930)
Girl with a Doll
Pen and ink and watercolour
27.5 × 21 cm (10⅞ × 8¼ in.)
Signed: *Pascin* (bottom right)
Stamped: *ATELIER PASCIN* (bottom right)
GR.180

Pablo Picasso (1881–1973)
Head of a Woman in Profile (Tête d'une femme en profile), from the 'Saltimbanques' suite
1905
Drypoint
29 × 25 cm (11½ × 9⅞ in.)
GR.181

Group of Three Women (Groupe de trois femmes)
ca. 1922–23
Drypoint and etching
17.5 × 12.5 cm (6⅞ × 5 in.)
Signed: *Picasso 88/100* (bottom margin)
GR.182
Plate 11

Filippo de Pisis (1896–1956)
Still Life with Bottles
1945
Oil on canvas
52 × 35 cm (20½ × 13¾ in.)
Signed and dated: *Pisis 45* (top left)
GR.183

Street Scene in Italy
ca. 1936
Oil on canvas
47.5 × 32 cm (18¾ × 12⅝ in.)
Signed: *Pisis* (bottom right)
GR.184

Camille Pissarro (1830–1903)
Portrait of Félix Pissarro (Portrait de Félix Pissarro)
1887
Pencil and charcoal
9.5 × 6 cm (3¾ × 2⅜ in.)
GR.185
Plate 90

Landscape, Eragny-sur-Epte
1890
Watercolour
12.5 × 17 cm (5 × 6¾ in.)
Signed and dated: *C. Pissarro 1890* (bottom right)
Inscribed: *no.2* (bottom left) and *Eragny* (bottom right)
GR.186
Plate 37

Paul-Emile as a Child (L'Enfant Paul-Emile)
1887
Pen and ink
10 × 7.5 cm (4 × 3 in.)
Stamped: *C P* (bottom left)
GR.187

Meadow and Mill at Osny (Prairie et moulin à Osny)
1885
Etching
18 × 24.5 cm (7⅛ × 9⅝ in.)
Stamped: *C P* (bottom left)
Inscribed: *7/18* (bottom right)
GR.188

Setting Sun (Soleil Couchant)
1879
Etching
14 × 17.5 cm (5⅝ × 6⅞ in.)
Signed: *C. Pissarro* (bottom right margin)
Inscribed: *No.2 Soleil Couchant* (bottom left margin)
GR.189

Figure Studies
Charcoal
28.5 × 14 cm (11¼ × 5⅝ in.)
Stamped: *CP* (bottom left)
GR.190

Follower of Pierre Paul Prud'hon (1758–1823)
Standing Female Nude
Pen and ink
15.75 × 9 cm (6¼ × 3⅝ in.)
GR.191

Pierre Puvis de Chavannes (1824–1898)
Study for The Sacred Grove (Première Pensée du Bois sacré)
ca. 1882–83
Charcoal on paper on canvas
57 × 117.5 cm (22½ × 46¼ in.)
Signed: *P. Puvis de Chavannes* (bottom left)
Inscribed: *Première pensée du bois sacré* (bottom left)
GR.192
Plate 13

Odilon Redon (1840–1916)
A Throw of the Dice (Un Coup de dès)
ca. 1900
Lithograph
31 × 24 cm (12¼ × 9½ in.)
Signed with the artist's monogram on the stone (bottom right)
GR.193
Plate 8

I Saw Above the Misty Outline of a Human Form (Je vis dessus le contour vaporeux d'une forme humaine),
Illustration for René Philipon's *La Maison Hautée*
1896
Lithograph
28 × 19 cm (11 × 7½ in.)
GR.194

Rembrandt van Rijn (1606–1669)
The Death of the Virgin
1639
Etching and drypoint
40.9 × 31.5 cm (16⅛ × 12⅜ in.)
Signed and dated on the plate: *Rembrandt 1639* (bottom left)
GR.195
Plate 112

The Agony in the Garden
ca. 1657
Etching and drypoint
11.5 × 8.5 cm (4½ × 3⅜ in.)
Signed on the plate: *Rembrandt* (bottom right)
GR.197

Pierre-Auguste Renoir (1841–1919)
The Country Dance (La Danse à la campagne)
1890
Etching
24 × 15 cm (9½ × 5⅞ in.)
Signed: *Renoir* (bottom right)
GR.198
Plate 96

The Olive Trees at Cagnes-sur-Mer (Les Oliviers à Cagnes-sur-Mer)
ca. 1903–19
Oil on canvas
13 × 11 cm (5⅛ × 4⅜ in.)
GR.199
Plate 35

Joshua Reynolds (1723–1792)
Lieutenant Haswell, RN
ca. 1746
Oil on canvas
46 × 36 cm (18⅛ × 14¼ in.)
Inscribed: *Master Haswell, Son of John Haswell of Tiverton, Devon* (reverse)
GR.200
Plate 47

George Richmond (1809–1896)
Two Portrait Sketches of Samuel Palmer
ca. 1825–35
Pen and ink
26.5 × 20 cm (10½ × 7⅞ in.)
GR.201
Plate 58

John Keble
Black and white chalk
14 × 12.5 cm (5½ × 5 in.)
GR.202

William Blake Richmond (1842–1921)
Profile Study of a Female Head
Black and white chalk
34 × 26 cm (13⅜ × 10¼ in.)
GR.203

Figure Study for the mosaic of the Delphic Sybil in St Paul's Cathedral, London
ca. 1890–1900
Black chalk
54.5 × 35.5 cm (21½ × 14 in.)
Inscribed: *Study for the Delphic Sybil for one of the spaces – the easternmost – flanking the clerestory windows on the north side of the choir* (top left)
GR.204

Louis Riesener (1808–1878)
Head of a Man
Coloured chalk
18 × 14.5 cm (7⅛ × 5¾ in.)
Stamped: *Vente Riesener* (bottom right)
GR.205

Chinese Peony
Watercolour
19.5 × 16.5 cm (7¾ × 6½ in.)
Stamped: *Vente Riesener* (bottom right)
GR.206

Auguste Rodin (1840–1917)
Nude Study
Watercolour and pencil
27 × 21.5 cm (10⅝ × 8½ in.)
Signed: *Rodin* (bottom right)
GR.208
Plate 1

George Romney (1734–1802)
The Little Scholar
Black chalk
17.25 × 11 cm (6⅞ × 4⅜ in.)
Stamped with a collector's mark: *adeP* (bottom right)
GR.209

Dante Gabriel Rossetti (1828–1882)
Portrait of Elizabeth Siddal, the Artist's Wife
ca. 1860
Pencil
23 × 19.5 cm (9⅛ × 7¾ in.)
GR.210
Plate 61

Georges Rouault (1871–1958)
Three Crosses (Trois Croix)
1938
Etching
32.5 × 24 cm (12⅞ × 9½ in.)
Signed and dated on the plate: *GR. 1938* (bottom right)
GR.211
Plate 117

Naked Woman (Femme nue) – Illustration for Baudelaire's Les Fleurs du Mal
1928
Etching
28 × 18.5 cm (11 × 7⅜ in.)
Signed on the plate: *GR. 1928* (bottom right)
GR.212

John Ruskin (1819–1900)
Lauffenbourg
ca. 1863
Pencil and pen and ink
31 × 40.5 cm (12¼ × 16 in.)
GR.215

Sally Ryan (1917–1968)
Small Flower Painting (Nasturtiums)
Oil on canvas
25.5 × 20.5 cm (10⅛ × 8⅛ in.)
Signed: *S.R.* (bottom right)
GR.216
Plate 69

Portrait of Kathleen
Oil on canvas
40.5 × 35.5 cm (16 × 14 in.)
GR.217

Poplars at Dulwich
1965
Oil on canvas
35.5 × 25.5 cm (14 × 10⅛ in.)
GR.218

The Cutting Garden,
Connecticut
1960
Oil on canvas
56 × 56 cm (22⅛ × 22⅛ in.)
Signed: *S.RYAN* (bottom right)
GR.219

Potted Plant
ca. 1967
Oil on canvas
61 × 46 cm (24 × 18⅛ in.)
GR.220

Winter Tree
Coloured chalk
55.5 × 44 cm (21⅞ × 17⅜ in.)
GR.221

Winter Afternoon, Walking
Home
1966
Coloured chalk
24.5 × 34 cm (9⅝ × 13⅜ in.)
GR.222

Attributed to Lorenzo
Salimbeni, known as Lorenzo
da San Severino (1374–ca.
1420)
An Angel of the Annunciation
Oil on panel
43 × 17.5 cm (16⅞ × 6⅞ in.)
GR.231
Plate 113

Emile Schuffenecker
(1851–1934)
Girl Knitting
Pencil
15 × 9.5 cm (5⅞ × 3¾ in.)
Stamped with the artist's
monogram (bottom right)
GR.232

Forrester Scott (?–1871)
Leicester Music Society
Pencil and white chalk
18.5 × 27.5 cm (7¾ × 10⅞ in.)
GR.233

Joseph Severn (1793–1879)
Portrait of a Man (said to be
John Keats)
Watercolour
12.5 × 10.5 cm (5 × 4⅛ in.)
GR.357

William Shackleton
(1872–1933)
Study for The Mackerel Nets
ca. 1913
Pencil
21 × 25 cm (8¼ × 9⅞ in.)
Signed: *W. Shackleton*
(bottom right)
GR.234

Ben Shahn (1898–1969)
Psalm 133 – Dove with
Painted Text
1960
Watercolour
26 × 17 cm (10¼ × 6¾ in.)
Signed: *Ben Shahn* (bottom
left)
GR.235
Plate 105

Walter Sickert (1860–1942)
San Marco, Venice
ca. 1895–1903
Pencil, black chalk and
watercolour
30 × 38 cm (11¾ × 14⅞ in.)
Signed: *Sickert* (bottom left)
GR.236
Plate 38

Alfred Sisley (1839–1899)
The Artist's Son, Pierre
1880
Pencil
23 × 31 cm (9⅛ × 12⅞ in.)
Inscribed: *Pierre 28 novembre*
1880 (bottom centre)
GR.237
Plate 92

Matthew Smith (1879–1959)
Flower Piece
ca. 1952–53
Oil on board
50.5 × 40 cm (19⅞ × 15¾ in.)
Signed: *M S* (bottom right)
GR.238
Plate 70

Fruit Bowl
Watercolour
21.5 × 32 cm (8½ × 12⅝ in.)
GR.239

Follower of Hendrick Sorgh
(ca. 1609/11–1670)
Studies of Peasants' Heads
Oil on canvas on panel
Each 7.5 × 7.5 cm (3 × 3 in.)
GR.240a and b

Follower of Pierre Subleyras
(1699–1749)
Hector Being Dragged Through
Troy
Oil on canvas
62.5 × 75 cm (24⅝ × 29½ in.)
GR.32

William Makepeace Thackeray
(1811–1863)
Self-Portrait
Pencil
19.5 × 14 cm (7¾ × 5⅝ in.)
Inscribed: *Avec les*
compliments de l'Auteur
(bottom right)
GR.242
Plate 56

Attributed to Titian
(ca. 1485/90–1576)
Angel (Putto)
Oil on paper on canvas
41 × 24.5 cm (16⅛ × 9⅝ in.)
GR.243

Constant Troyon (1810–1865)
Oxen with Cart
Black chalk
17 × 28 cm (6¾ × 11 in.)
Signed: *C. Troyon* (bottom left)
GR.244

Joseph Mallord William Turner
(1775–1851)
Carlisle
ca. 1797
Pen and ink and watercolour
11 × 16.5 cm (4⅜ × 6½ in.)
GR.245
Plate 41

Follower of Joseph Mallord
William Turner (1775–1851)
Clitheroe Castle
Watercolour
15.5 × 20.5 cm (6⅛ × 8⅛ in.)
GR.246

Studio of Paolo Veronese
(1528–1588)
Page Boy
Oil on canvas
137 × 71 cm (54 × 28 in.)
GR.247

Edouard Vuillard (1868–1940)
The Wet Nurse (La Nourrice)
Black chalk
23.5 × 16.5 cm (9¼ × 6½ in.)
Signed: *E.V.* (bottom left)
GR.248
Plate 102

James Ward (1769–1859)
An Ancient Oak
Watercolour
18 × 11.5 cm (7⅛ × 4½ in.)
Signed: *J.W.* (bottom left)
GR.249

Cow in a Barn
Oil on panel
27.5 × 35 cm (10⅞ × 13¾ in.)
Carved: *J.W.* (reverse)
GR.250

Frank Ward (1914–1998)
Portrait Study of a Little Girl
1946
Brown chalk
34 × 24.5 cm (13⅜ × 9⅝ in.)
Signed and dated: *F. Ward*
Sept 46 (bottom right)
GR.251

Follower of Antoine Watteau
(1684–1721)
Studies of Women in Three
Poses
Red and black chalk
23 × 35 cm (9⅛ × 13¾ in.)
GR.252

Alice Weldon (1944–)
Cyclamen
Pencil
31.5 × 27.5 cm (12⅜ × 10⅞ in.)
GR.358

Ian Seymour Wells (1937–)
Willow over a Stream
1972
Pencil
16 × 25 cm (6¾ × 9⅞ in.)
Signed and dated: *I.S.W. 72*
(bottom left)
Inscribed: *Willow over Stream*
nr. Salisbury (bottom left)
GR.253

Figure Study Outdoors
1971
Black chalk, pen and ink and
watercolour
18.5 × 12 cm (7¾ × 4¾ in.)
Signed and dated: *I.S.W. 71*
(top right)
GR.254

Sleeping Girl – Vicky
1970
Black chalk
21.5 × 27.5 cm (8½ × 5⅞ in.)
Signed: *I.S.W. 70* (bottom
right)
Inscribed: *Vicky* (bottom right)
GR.255

Richard Westall (1765–1836)
Lady Charles Harvey
Pencil, pen and ink,
watercolour and gouache
14 × 12 cm (5⅝ × 4¾ in.)
GR.256

**James Abbott McNeill Whistler
(1834–1903)**
*The Adam and Eve, Old
Chelsea*
1878
Etching
17 × 29.5 cm (6¾ × 11⅝ in.)
Stamped with the artist's
butterfly 'signature' (bottom
margin)
GR.257

Peter de Wint (1784–1849)
Turnips
Watercolour
13 × 15.5 cm (5⅛ × 6⅛ in.)
GR.258

Michael Wishart (1928–1996)
Arab Courtyard, Fez
1971
Oil on canvas
39.5 × 49.5 cm (15⅝ × 19½ in.)
Signed and dated: *Wishart 71*
(bottom right)
GR.259

Moths on a Blue Path
1963
Oil on canvas
50 × 75 cm (19¾ × 29½ in.)
Signed and dated: *MW 63*
(bottom right)
GR.260
Plate 34

**Follower of Domenico
Zampieri, known as
Domenichino (1581–1641)**
*Head of a Young Man Looking
Upwards*
Black chalk
27.5 × 20 cm (10⅞ × 7⅞ in.)
GR.42

SCULPTURE AND APPLIED ART

Cameroonian (Bamileke Kingdom)
Royal stool
ca. 1920s–30s
Wood
Height 49 cm (19³/₈ in.)
Diameter 42 cm (16⁵/₈ in.)
GR.321
Plate 21

William Chattaway (1927–)
Douglas Garman
1964
Bronze
Height 26 cm (10¹/₄ in.)
Signed and dated: *Chattaway '64 1/6*
GR.19

Chinese
Incense burner in the shape of a tortoise
Sung Dynasty, *ca.* 960–1279
Length 19 cm (7¹/₂ in.)
GR.303
Plate 75

Figurine of a pony with a monkey on its back
Late Ming Dynasty,
ca. 1500–1644
Length 5 cm (2 in.)
GR.304

Figurine of a man
Northern Wei Dynasty,
ca. 386–535
Greystone, with traces of slip and red pigment
Height 33 cm (13 in.)
GR.305

Figurine of a horseman – from a group of funerary figures
Northern Wei Dynasty,
ca. 6th century
Greystone
Height 23 cm (8¹/₈ in.)
GR.306

Vase with dragon-head handles
Tang Dynasty, early 8th century
Terracotta with green, brown and white glazes
Height 35.5 cm (14 in.)
GR.307

Head of a Bodhisattva (from Longmen, Henan Province)
ca. 6th–7th century
Limestone
Height 13.5 cm (5³/₈ in.)
GR.308

Conical bowl
Northern Song Dynasty,
ca. 960–1279
Clay
Diameter 24 cm (9¹/₂ in.)
GR.351

Congolese
Cup
ca. 19th–20th century
Ivory
Height 29.5 cm (11⁵/₈ in.)
GR.330

Dalmatian
Fragment of a reliquary cross
ca. 1400
Brass
Length 18.5 cm (7³/₈ in.)
GR.345

Edgar Degas (1834–1917)
Woman Washing her Left Leg (Femme se lavant sa jambe gauche)
1895; cast *ca.* 1919–21
Bronze
Height 14.5 cm (5³/₄ in.)
Signed: *Degas*
Inscribed: *no.17* (serial number) *HER.D.* (set mark)
GR.34
Plate 5

Egyptian
Head of a girl
ca. 1987–1640 BC
Limestone, with traces of paint
Height 12 cm (4³/₄ in.)
GR.261

Sculptor's trial piece for a head of a lion
Late Period, *ca.* 712–730 BC
Limestone
Height 10 cm (4 in.)
GR.262

Jar with slender ovoid body, ring neck and two handles
Early Dynastic Period,
ca. 2965–2705 BC
Alabaster
Height 12.5 cm (5 in.)
GR.263

Jar with slender ovoid body and ring neck
Early Dynastic Period,
ca. 2965–2705 BC
Alabaster
Height 12.5 cm (5 in.)
GR.264
Plate 67

Vase with ovoid body, flattened rim and two lug handles
Pre-Dynastic, *ca.* 3300–3000 BC
Diorite
Height 15 cm (5⁷/₈ in.)
GR.265

Bowl with a large flat rim
Pre-Dynastic, *ca.* 3500–3200 BC
Diorite
Diameter 6 cm (2³/₈ in.)
GR.266

Green glazed vase with two handles, decorated with a frieze of blue glaze leaves
Roman period, *ca.* 1st century BC–1st century AD
Clay
Height 12 cm (4³/₄ in.)
GR.267

Cosmetic jar with circular body
Stone
Diameter 10.5 cm (4¹/₈ in.)
GR.268

Vase, decorated with a boat scene
Pre-Dynastic, *ca.* 3500–3000 BC
Clay
Height 18 (7¹/₈ in.)
GR.269

Green and blue glazed
cosmetic jar in the shape of a
column, decorated with lotus
plants and a monkey
New Kingdom, *ca.* 1540–
1075 BC
Faïence
Height 6.5 cm (2⅝ in.)
GR.270

Cosmetic jar
Middle Kingdom, 12th Dynasty,
ca. 1938–1759 BC
Blue marble
Height 5.5 cm (2¼ in.)
GR.271

*Cosmetic jar supported by a
figure of a monkey*
ca. 600–300 BC
Steatite
Height 7 cm (2¾ in.)
GR.272

Frog
New Kingdom, *ca.* 1540–
1075 BC
Serpentine
Length 9 cm (3⅝ in.)
GR.273

Falcon
Late Period 712–730 BC
Bronze
Height 11 cm (4⅜ in.)
GR.274

Head of Akhenaten
ca. 1450 BC
Stone
Length 11 cm (4⅜ in.)
GR.275

*Relief of a servant paying
homage to his king, from Tel-
el-Armarna*
18th Dynasty, 1350–1300 BC
Limestone, with traces of paint
20 × 25 cm (7⅞ × 9⅞ in.)
GR.276

*Figure of a standing man
wearing a short wig*
ca. 2500–2200 BC
Wood
Height 20 cm (7⅞ in.)
GR.277

*Horus in the form of
Harpocrates, wearing the
uraeus and the lock of eternal
youth*
Saite Period, *ca.* 664–525 BC
Bronze
Height 12.5 cm (5 in.)
GR.278

*The goddess Neith, wearing
the red crown of honour*
Saite Period, *ca.* 664–525 BC
Bronze
Height 21 cm (8¼ in.)
GR.279

A blue glazed figure of a hawk
Late Period, *ca.* 712–730 BC
Faïence
Height 7 cm (2⅝ in.)
GR.280

*A figure of a woman with the
uraeus and a lotus capital on
her head*
Late Period, *ca.* 1000–300 BC
Wood
Height 24 cm (9½ in.)
GR.281

*Mask, believed to be of Queen
Nefertiti*
18th Dynasty, 1350–1300 BC
Plaster
Height 17 cm (6¾ in.)
GR.360
Plate 55

Head of a woman
18th Dynasty, 1350–1300 BC
Limestone
Height 20 cm (7⅞ in.)
GR.361

Georg Ehrlich (1897–1966)
Head of a Deer
ca. 1957–58
Bronze
Height 32 cm (12⅝ in.)
Signed: *EHRLICH*
GR.47
Plate 78

Seated Boy
1948
Bronze
Height 20.5 cm (8⅛ in.)
GR.48

English (Nottingham)
Resurrection
15th century
Alabaster
38 × 27 cm (15 × 10⅝ in.)
GR.349
Plate 108

Jacob Epstein (1880–1959)
*Third Portrait of Esther with
Flower*
1949
Bronze
Height 62 cm (24½ in.)
GR.77
Plate 45

*First Portrait of Kitty (with
curls)*
1944
Bronze
Height 38 cm (15 in.)
GR.78

Bust of Meum
1918
Bronze
Height 42 cm (16⅝ in.)
GR.79
Plate 54

*The Sisters (Anne and Annabel
Freud)*
ca. 1952
Bronze
Height 18.5 cm (7⅜ in.)
GR.80
Plate 82

St Francis
1942
Bronze
Height 31 cm (12¼ in.)
GR.81

Mask of Rabindranath Tagore
1926
Bronze
Height 50.8 cm (20 in.)
Signed: *Epstein* (on back)
GR.82
Plate 53

Baby Awake
ca. 1902–04
Bronze
Height 18.5 cm (7⅜ in.)
GR.83

Study of a Cat
ca. 1920
Bronze
Height 17 cm (6¾ in.)
Length 30 cm (11⅞ in.)
GR.84

Roland Joffé
ca. 1949–50
Bronze
Height 21 cm (8¼ in.)
GR.85

Frisky, the Artist's Dog
1953
Bronze
Height 31 cm (12¼ in.)
GR.86
Plate 79

Nan, the Dreamer
1911
Bronze
Height 28 cm (11 in.)
Length 35.5cm (14 in.)
GR.87

First Portrait of Kathleen
1921
Bronze
Height 47 cm (18½ in.)
GR.88

T.S. Eliot
1951
Bronze
Height 47 cm (18½ in.)
GR.89

Hands of the Risen Christ
1917–19
Bronze
Height 31 cm (12¼ in.)
GR.90

*Maquette for Cavendish
Square Madonna and Child*
1950
Lead, halo in bronze
Height 35 cm (13¾ in.)
GR.91
Plate 109

Sally Ryan
1937
Bronze
Height 39 cm (15⅜ in.)
GR.354

Heads of New York Madonna
and Child
ca. 1926–27
Bronze
Height 48.2 cm (19 in.)
GR.362

First Portrait of Esther (with
long hair)
1944
Bronze
Height 46 cm (18⅛ in.)
GR.363
Plate 81

Etruscan
Figure of a youth
7th–5th century BC
Bronze
Height 9 cm (3⅝ in.)
GR.301

Etruscan/Roman
Ladle, with the finial shaped
into a wolf's head
5th–1st century BC
Bronze
Length 27 cm (10⅝ in.)
GR.302

European
Pair of praying hands
ca. 12th–18th century
Marble
Length 27 cm (10⅝ in.)
GR.342

Two Embroidered Stoles
16th century
Length of both 97 cm
(38¼ in.)
GR.344

Flemish (Malines/Mechelen)
St Jerome in the Wilderness
16th century
Alabaster
12 × 9 cm (4¾ × 3⅝ in.)
GR.343

French
Christ with the Crown of
Thorns
ca. 12th–14th century
Wood
Height 36.5 cm (14⅜ in.)
GR.346
Plate 114

Figure of a monk with a book
Terracotta
Height 60 cm (23⅝ in.)
GR.350

**Henri Gaudier-Brzeska
(1891–1915)**
Women Bearing Sacks
1912
Plaster
36 × 28 cm (14¼ × 11 in.)
Signed with artist's monogram
(bottom right)
GR.122
Plate 101

Ghanaian (Ashante people)
Kuduo box with geometric
patterning
ca. 19th–20th century
Bronze
Length 7 cm (2⅝ in.)
GR.329

Greek
Head of a Youth
Hellenistic Period, ca. 4th–1st
century BC
Clay
Height 10 cm (4 in.)
GR.282

Vase (lekythos) depicting
warriors in combat, watched
by an aristocratic man
ca. 6th century BC
Clay
Height 15 cm (5⅞ in.)
GR.284

Cockerel
ca. 4th century BC
Terracotta, with painted details
Height 16.5 cm (6½ in.)
GR.286

Europa and the bull (from
Boetia)
ca. 6th–4th century BC
Terracotta
Height 15.5 cm (6⅛ in.)
GR.287

Bull
ca. 4th–3rd century BC
Terracotta
Length 11 cm (4¼ in.)
GR.288

Figure of a woman with a
cloak
ca. 4th–3rd century BC
Terracotta
Height 27.5 cm (10¾ in.)
GR.289

Figurine of a young man in
the style of a Kouros
ca. 6th century BC
Bronze
Height 8.5 cm (3⅜ in.)
GR.290

Bird
4th century BC
Terracotta, with traces of
colour slip
Height 7 cm (2¾ in.)
GR.291

Bird
4th century BC
Terracotta, with traces of
colour slip
Height 7 cm (2¾ in.)
GR.292

Head of a woman
Late Hellenistic Period,
ca. 2nd–1st century BC
Terracotta
Height 8.5 cm (3⅜ in.)
GR.338

Indian
The Goddess Parvati and
attendants (from North Central
India)
ca. 11th–12th century
Sandstone
Height 27 cm (10⅝ in.)
GR.323
Plate 118

Covered box
Mughal period, ca. 1526–1761
Rock crystal
Diameter 6 cm (2⅜ in.)
GR.327

Italian
Figurine of Hercules
ca. 17th–18th century
Bronze
Height 15.5 cm (6¼ in.)
GR.141

Figurine of a bearded man (in
antique style)
ca. 17th century
Bronze
Height 11.5 cm (4½ in.)
GR.283

Head of a lion
ca. 17th–19th century
Brass alloy
Length 17.5 cm (6⅞ in.)
GR.295

Figurine of Diana
ca. 17th–19th century
Bronze
Height 10.5 cm (4 ⅛ in.)
GR.300

Head of a female saint
ca. 19th century
Mosaic
Length 7 cm (2¾ in.)
GR.340

Mitre
17th century
Copper, gilt and inlaid
coloured stones
Height 26.0cm (10¼ in.)
GR.348

Torso (from Southern Italy)
12th–13th century
Marble
Height 42 cm (16⅝ in.)
GR.353

Ivory Coast
Heddle pulley from an upright
loom
ca. 19th–20th century
Wood
Length 22 cm (8¾ in.)
GR.332
Plate 14

Mesopotamian
Double bull's head (from
Sumeria)
ca. 3000–2500 BC
Steatite
Length 7.5 cm (3 in.)
GR.316

Socketed axe (from Sumeria)
ca. 4000–3000 BC
Bronze
Length 9 cm (3½ in.)
GR.317

Duck weight
ca. 3000–2000 BC
Magnelite
Length 4.5 cm (1¾ in.)
GR.318

Duck weight
ca. 3000–2000 BC
Bronze
Length 5.5 cm (2¼ in.)
GR.319

Mexican (Pre-Columbian – Toltec people)
Figurine of a man
ca. 1000–1200
Obsidian
Height 8.5 cm (3⅜ in.)
GR.337

Minoan
Vase with two handles
Middle Minoan, *ca.* 1650 BC
Stone
Diameter 9.5 cm (3¾ in.)
GR.293

New Guinean (Latmul or Abelan peoples)
New Guinean
comb (from Southern Coast or Torres Strait)
ca. 19th–20th century
Wood
Length 34 cm (13⅜ in.)
GR.331
Plate 15

Box in the shape of a crocodile with a bird's head at the tail
Probably 20th century
Wood
Length 33 cm (13 in.)
GR.334

New Zealand (Maori people)
Hei-Tiki
Greenstone with mother-of-pearl inlaid eyes
Length 12.5 cm (5 in.)
GR.324
Plate 17

Nicobar Islands
Kareau
ca. 19th–20th century
Wood
Length 17.5 cm (6⅞ in.)
GR.333

Northwest American (Inuit people)
Three figurines of seals
ca. 20th century
Walrus ivory
Lengths 8.5 cm (3⅜ in.), 8 cm (3⅛ in.) and 5.5 cm (2¼ in.)
GR.328

Ottoman
Dish with the centre embossed with a figure of St John the Baptist
ca. 19th–20th century
Silver
Diameter 27 cm (10⅝ in.)
GR.341

Persian (Luristan)
Finial in the shape of a head of an ibex
ca. 850–650 BC
Bronze
Length 11 cm (4⅜ in.)
GR.312
Plate 74

Handle in the shape of a horse
Sassanian Dynasty,
ca. AD 224–651
Bronze
Length 10 cm (4 in.)
GR.313

Turquoise bowl
Sassanian Dynasty,
ca. 224–651 AD
Clay with turquoise glaze
Diameter 9 cm (3⅝ in.)
GR.315
Plate 64

Votive tube, decorated with a female figure (from Luristan)
ca. 850–650 BC
Bronze
Height 12.5 cm (5 in.)
GR.320

Peruvian (Mochican people)
Vessel in the form of a man's head, with the top painted with a frieze of running animals
ca. AD 400–600
Clay
Height 19.5 cm (7¾ in.)
GR.335
Plate 52

Spouted bottle with linear decoration
ca. AD 400–600
Clay
Height 19 cm (7½ in.)
GR.336

Polynesian
Two shell ornaments with geometric patterns
ca. 19th–20th century
Shell
Lengths 12 cm (4¾ in.) and 12.5 cm (5 in.)
GR.326

Queen Charlotte Islands (Haida people)
Eagle
ca. 19th–early 20th century
Whalebone
Height 33 cm (13 in.)
GR.322
Plate 80

Auguste Rodin (1840–1917)
Mask of a Woman
Bronze
Height 12.5 cm (5 in.)
GR.207

Roman
Head of a mourning woman
1st century AD
Marble, mounted on a marble plinth
Height 30 cm (11⅞ in.)
GR.285
Plate 4

Head of a laughing boy
ca. 1st–2nd century AD
Marble
Height 17 cm (6¾ in.)
GR.294

Fragment of a hand
ca. 1st–2nd century AD
Marble
Length 13.5 cm (5⅜ in.)
GR.296

Pair of marble feet
ca. 500 BC–AD 500
Marble
Length 17 cm (6¾ in.)
GR.297

Fragment of a relief, depicting a satyr
ca. 1st century BC–3rd century AD
Terracotta
Length 16 cm (6⅜ in.)
GR.298
Plate 16

Decoration for a jug in the shape of an actor's mask
ca. 1st century BC–1st century AD
Copper alloy and silver inlay
Height 5 cm (2 in.)
GR.299

Vase in the shape of a youth's head
ca. 1st century BC–1st century AD
Clay
Height 24 cm (9½ in.)
GR.314

Sally Ryan (1916–1968)
Head of a Girl with Curls
Bronze
Height 32 cm
GR.223

The Martinique
1934
Bronze
Height 31 cm (12½ in.)
Signed: *Sally Ryan 1934*
GR.224

Nathaniel
Bronze
Height 32 cm (12⅝ in.)
GR.225
Plate 83

Head of a Girl in a Chinese Jacket
Bronze
Height 35 cm (13¾ in.)
GR.226

Head of Valentina
Bronze
Height 32 cm (12⅝ in.)
GR.227

W. Somerset Maugham
Plaster
Height 34 cm (13⅜ in.)
GR.228

Unfinished Mask
Marble
Height 31 cm (12¼ in.)
GR.229

Mother and Child
Limestone
Height 50 cm (19¾ in.)
GR.230
Plate 89

Solomon Islands
Food bowl
ca. 19th–20th century
Wood
Length 94 cm (37 in.)
GR.352

Siamese
Head of the youthful Buddha
ca. 18th–19th century
Bronze with gilt
Height 15 cm (5⅞ in.)
GR.309

Hand raised with palm forwards in the gesture of Abhaya Mudra (assurance, blessing and protection)
Early 20th century
Bronze
Height 20 cm (7⅞ in.)
GR.310

Figurine of the Buddha
ca. 1750–1850
Gold and silver
Height 13.5 cm (5⅜ in.)
GR.311

Sierra Leone (Mende people)
Head
ca. 19th–20th century
Stone
Length 12.5 cm (5 in.)
GR.325

Spanish
Figurine of Christ holding a lamb
Late 16th century
Alabaster
Height 11 cm (4⅜ in.)
GR.339

Figure of Christ with outstretched arms
17th century
Wood
Height 85 cm (33½ in.)
GR.347

WORKS ON LONG-TERM LOAN FROM KITTY GODLEY

Jacob Epstein (1880–1959)
Second Portrait of Kitty
1947
Bronze
Height 31.5 cm (13 in.)

Old Pinager's Clasped Hands
1923
Bronze
Height 14 cm (5½ in.)

The Hon. Robert Hesketh
1956
Bronze
Height 40 cm (15½ in.)

David Lloyd George
1959
Bronze
Height 24 cm (9½ in.)

Select Bibliography

Bernard Van Dieren, *Epstein*, London and New York 1920

Arnold Haskell, *The Sculptor Speaks: Jacob Epstein to Arnold L. Haskell. A Series of Conversations on Art*, London 1931

L.B. Powell, *Jacob Epstein*, London 1932

Jacob Epstein, *Let There Be Sculpture: An Autobiography*, London 1940; republished as *Epstein: An Autobiography*, London 1955

Geoffrey Ireland, *Jacob Epstein: A Camera Study of the Sculptor at Work*, London 1958

Richard Buckle, *Jacob Epstein, Sculptor*, London 1963

Richard Buckle and Kathleen Epstein, *Epstein Drawings*, London 1963

Michael Wishart, *High Diver*, London 1977

Evelyn Silber, *The Sculpture of Epstein*, Oxford 1986

Jacob Epstein: Sculpture and Drawings, exhib. cat. by Evelyn Silber and Terry Friedman, London, Whitechapel Art Gallery, April–June 1987; Leeds, The Henry Moore Centre for the Study of Sculpture and Leeds City Art Galleries, July–September 1987

Ezio Bassani and Malcolm D. McLeod, *Jacob Epstein, Collector*, Milan 1989

Stephen Gardiner, *Epstein: Artist Against the Establishment*, London 1992

Picture Credits

Frontispiece photo: Hélène Binet

Essay figures
Fig. 11   Photo: E.M. Chester Studio
Fig. 18   Photo: Paul Laib, Leeds Museums and Galleries (Henry Moore Institute)
Fig. 19   Photo: Geoffrey Ireland
Fig. 24   Photo: Larkfield Photography, Brighouse
Fig. 25   Photopress
Fig. 26   The Metropolitan Museum of Art, New York
Fig. 27   Photo: Pierre V. Manevy from Black Star, Cliffords Inn, London
Fig. 33   Photo: Mary Evans Picture Library, London

Catalogue plates
11   © Succession Picasso/DACS 1999
38   © Estate of Walter Sickert, 1999. All Rights Reserved, DACS
39   © ADAGP, Paris, and DACS, London, 1999
42   © Succession H. Matisse/DACS 1999
62   © L&M SERVICES B.V. Amsterdam 990805
76   © ADAGP, Paris, and DACS, London, 1999
100   © ADAGP, Paris, and DACS, London, 1999
102   © ADAGP, Paris, and DACS, London, 1999
105   © Estate of Ben Shahn/VAGA, New York/ DACS, London, 1999
117   © ADAGP, Paris, and DACS, London, 1999

Page 112   © Bridgeman Artist's Copyright Service

Photography of the Garman Ryan Collection by Gary Kirkham; plates 9, 10, 22, 46, 61 and 85 by Anthony Barthorpe.